Be the Bird

Grow. Leap. Soar.

E. C. "ACE" Andersen

Be the Bird
Grow. Leap. Soar.

For information about permissions, inquiries, or bulk purchases, please contact:
Info@Acetrology.com

ISBN: 979-8-218-79198-8

This book is intended for informational and inspirational purposes only. It is not a substitute for professional advice, diagnosis, or treatment. Always seek the guidance of a qualified professional with any questions you may have regarding your mental, emotional, physical, or spiritual health. The author makes no guarantees about the applicability or effectiveness of the ideas presented herein for your specific circumstances, and you assume full responsibility for how you choose to apply this material.

This book is a work of creative nonfiction. Unless otherwise indicated, all stories, characters, and events are drawn from the author's personal experience and observation. Any resemblance to real persons, living or dead, is purely coincidental where not otherwise noted.

Cover design by Thomas Terrazas, TMT Graphics
Printed in the United States of America

First Edition

About the Cover

The cover of Be the Bird was brought to life by **Thomas Terrazas**. The colors are derived from my aura photograph, and both a statue and sunset in Sedona, AZ. Thomas is a gifted graphic designer, visionary artist, and someone whose creative fingerprints have graced many chapters of my life.

Our story began over two decades ago, when I was launching a community magazine and found myself in search of a standout designer. I called a local graphic design school and asked the director a simple question: "Is there anyone you'd personally recommend?" Without hesitation, they named Thomas. I reached out, and from our first collaboration, it was clear, I hadn't just found a designer, I had found a creative ally for life.

Since then, our paths have continued to intertwine through multiple ventures, evolutions, and visions. Through each twist of my journey, Thomas has brought not only his artistic skill but his unwavering loyalty, insight, and intuitive grasp of whatever dream I was breathing life into. He shows up, again and again, with quiet brilliance and a heart full of devotion, not just to the work, but to the spirit behind it.

He is a talented artist, a deeply devoted father, and someone I trust implicitly. That trust is etched into every curve and color of this cover. It's more than design, it's a reflection of two decades of shared growth, vision, and flight.

Thank you, Thomas, for breathing air into Be the Bird to help it soar.

Contents

SECTION 1: Seeing the Cage 1

SECTION 2: The Molting Season   15

SECTION 3: Nest, Feathers, and the Flock   41

SECTION 4: The Wind   59

Final Feathers

Acknowledgements

To Alex, Imagine gazing at the night sky for years, searching, wondering, and then witnessing a star being born before your eyes. With it comes awe, wonder, joy...responsibility, and perhaps even a little fear, but most of all, a profound sense of *why*. You are that star. You are that why. Your light has illuminated corners of my heart I didn't even know were waiting, and your presence reminds me what it means to believe in something bigger than myself. Thank you for being the brilliant, unexpected spark that gave all the waiting meaning.

To Robin, For a lifetime of unwavering love and support, reaching back before I was even old enough to remember. The irony is both beautiful and humbling, and surely no coincidence, that the oldest book I own is a signed children's book from you, given before I could even read. Or knew what a book was. You have been the most constant and steadfast presence in my life, quietly, patiently, and unfailingly there, becoming even more of a constant presence than Grandma and Grandpa in that sacred role. Thank you for seeing me, holding space, and showing up in ways both visible and invisible, time and again. You've been a cornerstone in my story, and I am profoundly grateful.

To Matt and April, for being a safe harbor and a solid foundation through the turbulence and challenges of our journey. Your warmth, steadiness, and open-heartedness gave me a place to land when I needed it most. Thank you for holding space for me to find my footing and for reminding me that I never had to face the storm alone. Your presence has been both a refuge and a guide, and I am deeply grateful.

To Denton, For quite literally making this book possible. For your openness, your willingness to jump on board without hesitation, and your steady hand in helping move this train down the track. Your faith in my vision and your readiness to help bring it to life mean more than words can fully express. Thank you for being part of the journey.

To the other Alex, Your enduring, boundless generosity, of time, insight, and spirit, has been a steady source of strength and clarity on this journey. Your consistent support, wisdom, and our many meaningful conversations have been an immeasurable treasure to me, far beyond what words can truly capture. Thank you for showing up, again and again, with an open mind and an even bigger heart.

To the countless souls, Whose kindness, wisdom, encouragement, and presence have touched my life in ways both profound and subtle, thank you. Whether through a quiet word, a shared moment, a hard-earned lesson, or simply by walking alongside me for a season, your support has shaped who I am and helped carry me to this point.

The list of names is far too long to fit on these pages, but please know that your contributions are neither forgotten nor diminished by their absence here. Each of you holds a place in my heart and in the fabric of this journey. If our paths have crossed, and you've offered help, guidance, or even a glimmer of kindness, know that I carry it with me still, remembered, appreciated, and woven into the wings that have lifted me higher.

Author's Note: Coming Full Circle

When I first read Viktor Frankl's *Man's Search for Meaning*, I didn't know it would follow me for decades. I didn't know that single line, *"Those who have a 'why' to live can bear with almost any 'how.'"* would become both a guide and a challenge for me.

At the time, I thought I understood it. But life has a way of testing what you *think* you know.

Over the years, I've lost things I thought I couldn't live without. I've faced storms I didn't believe I could withstand. And each time, when I felt myself faltering, I'd return to that idea: if I could find even a *sliver* of meaning, some reason to take the next step, I could keep going.

This book, and the journey that shaped it, has been my way of finding and articulating that *why*.

And now, I offer it to you.

You don't have to have it all figured out. You don't have to know the whole plan, or see the whole sky. You just have to be willing to ask the question: *Why?*

Not the shallow "why me?" of despair, but the deeper, braver *why* that looks for meaning even here, even now.

If you take nothing else from these pages, let it be this:
Your *why* exists.
It has always been there, waiting for you to uncover it.
And it will carry you farther than you ever imagined.

And to those whose love and light helped me find my way here, you'll find your generosity, and my gratitude, in the pages that follow.

So go ahead. Ask the question.
And trust that the answer, when you're ready to hear it, will rise to meet you, like a wind beneath your wings.
~ E. C. "ACE" Andersen

An Invitation to Take Flight

This book isn't here to fix you, because you were never broken.

It's a mirror.
A companion.
A quiet hand on your shoulder reminding you what you already know deep down:
You've always had wings. You've just been waiting for the right moment to trust them.

This is an invitation.

An invitation to see more clearly, to notice the cage you've outgrown, the stones you've carried too long, the songs that still live in your bones.
To gently set down what no longer belongs to you.
To ask the kind of questions that open doors, not close them.
To hear your own heart through all the noise.
To walk, or crawl or dance, toward who you are becoming.

Maybe... you're here because something inside you is already shifting.
Maybe you've known for a while that it's time.

This book is for the ones who feel the quiet ache of "more" even if they can't name it yet.
For the ones who've been holding it all together for everyone else.
For the ones whose light has dimmed under the weight of old stories, but who are starting to remember they were born to shine.
For the fierce, the tender, the tired, the ready.
For those willing to pause, look gently inward, and listen for truth beneath the noise.
This isn't about becoming someone else.
It's about returning.

Softening.
Stretching.
Trusting.
Flying.

If any part of this stirs something in you, then you are exactly who this book is for.

Welcome.
You've made it to the branch.
The sky is waiting.

Introduction

I didn't read a book cover to cover until I was in my early twenties.

Yes, that means I became skilled at skimming, reading summaries, and scanning tables of contents just enough to scrape by on book reports. It wasn't that I wasn't interested in books. I desperately wanted to glean the kind of insights I saw others finding in page after page.

But it was painful.

I struggled to settle in, to comprehend, to retain what I read. Paragraph after paragraph would slip through my mind like water through a sieve, and I'd find myself rereading whole sections, frustrated and defeated.

In high school, when we were assigned multiple chapters of reading homework, I remember the sinking, gut-wrenching feeling every time:
First, knowing I wasn't going to finish the assignment.
Second, dreading the inevitable report card that would reflect all those undiscovered chapters.

The first book I actually finished was on personal development, and I was hooked.

From that point forward, I read voraciously, though mostly personal development, because my academic self-esteem had been worn thin by years of trying to fit into a rigid system.

I was especially inspired by Tony Robbins, who achieved remarkable success despite not having followed the traditional path of school and career.

Reading never came easily, but I kept at it. Once, determined to prove to myself I could, I read Think and Grow Rich in a single 24-hour stretch, inspired by someone who claimed to have done the same. I have returned to that book many times since, and though my original intent was to unlock financial freedom, the book gave me something far richer.

It introduced me to the concept of manifestation, and opened my eyes to ideas about energy and vibration that were hidden beneath the surface of its words.

From then on, my love of learning only grew. I read constantly, so much so that I eventually had to stop visiting bookstores because I couldn't afford to bring home all the books I wanted. Then I discovered audiobooks, which allowed me to continue learning, even while working.

Looking back, I believe the books I've read in the years since far outweigh the ones I missed in academia.

I share this with you because I have a profound respect for those who have written the books that shaped my intellect, for the minds and souls that poured their wisdom, experience, and insight into pages so that others, like me, could explore and discover.

The ideas in this book are not mine alone. They arise from a lifetime of study, reflection, and practice, built upon the wisdom of many who came before me. I have only rearranged, reinterpreted, distilled and delivered the truths I've discovered in a way that I hope feels accessible and meaningful to you.

This book is my way of passing those insights forward, of offering something that might not otherwise have found its way to you.

It is also intended to serve as a foundation and primer, especially for anyone who chooses to work with me directly.

Writing this book, and doing the inner work it reflects, has felt a lot like that old story about the builder who creates, not only for his own path but for the ones who will walk it after him.

I've always loved that image: of a quiet traveler, pausing to build a bridge he'll never cross again, not because he needs it, but because someone else will.

May my journey serve yours, and may this book meet you where you need it most.

What's Inside This Book

This book is a collection of the lessons, metaphors, and practices that helped me learn to trust myself and my own wings.

Each chapter explores a different principle, from knowing yourself, to navigating change, to raising your energy, finding your voice, and learning to fly when the branch you're standing on breaks.

You'll find stories, reflections, affirmations, exercises, and questions to help you integrate what you read.

You don't need to read this book all at once, and you don't need to agree with everything in it. Take what resonates.

Pause when you need to. Return to certain chapters as they call to you.

My hope is that these pages offer you not just insight, but also practical ways to embody what you already carry within: your own confidence, your own truth, your own wings.

Wherever you are on your journey, I invite you to walk through these chapters with curiosity, openness, self-compassion, and to discover, step by step, what has been waiting for you all along.

This book is a map and a mirror, to guide and reflect.

The Mystical Properties of Birds,

A Reflection for Be the Bird

Across cultures and centuries, birds have served as messengers, symbols, and guides, appearing in myths, dreams, and sacred texts as bridges between earth and sky. Their ability to lift off from the ground with ease has long inspired a sense of wonder, representing liberation from earthly burdens and access to higher perspective.

Birds are more than just animals of flight, they are emblems of:

- **Freedom** - The open sky is their home. They remind us we are not confined by old stories or limits others have placed on us.

- **Perspective** - From above, everything looks different. What once felt overwhelming or impossible can shrink in scale when we change our vantage point.

- **Transition** - Feathers, molting, migration—all speak to cycles of growth, letting go, and returning changed.

- **Spiritual messages** - Birds are often said to carry the messages of the divine, showing up as synchronicities, omens, or confirmations.

- **Awakening** - Their songs often mark the beginning of a new day. In this way, birds signal rebirth and new chapters.

In *Be the Bird*, the symbolism is both literal and spiritual.

You are invited to step into the mystical essence of the bird, to **become** the one who sings at dawn, who leaves the nest, who trusts the wind even when the branch breaks.

The bird is not just a concept in the book.
It is you.
Your story.
Your flight.
Your remembering.

SECTION 1: SEEING THE CAGE

Before we can take flight, we must first see what holds us. This section invites you to gently notice the invisible bars, the patterns of nature, nurture, and experience, that have shaped your inner cage. Here you will learn to name the codes you've inherited, to listen to the guidance of your emotions, and to recognize the loops and weights that keep you circling. Awareness is the first opening in the bars.

The Caged Bird

Freeing ourselves starts with acknowledging the bars. Our nature, the blueprint we're born with, and our nurture, the world that shapes us, together build the structure of our cage.

These bars, written in our DNA, shaped by our families, etched by our earliest memories, form the invisible walls that surround us. They shape what we see, what we believe we can reach. And yet, even here, the bird still sings.

When we think about our nature, we're considering our blueprint. Science has revealed fascinating aspects of who we are through DNA and genome sequencing. These complex codes shape everything from our eye color to our physicality, temperament, and even certain predispositions. The intricacies of biology are astounding, and no two people are exactly alike. Statistically, the odds of two people being identical are in the trillions. Just consider fingerprints: no two ever recorded have been the same.

And yet, amid all these differences, we share undeniable similarities. We all bleed. We all breathe. And no matter our biology or beliefs, we all experience thoughts and emotions.

At some point during pregnancy, our thoughts and emotional imprint begin to form. Even in the womb, we are shaped by what our mothers eat, how well they sleep, the music they hear, and the emotional states they carry. Those early influences integrate with our natural blueprint before we even take our first breath.

Then a stork visits annnd... we're born.

We enter the world carrying inherited tendencies, energetic imprints, and ancestral patterns, then immediately begin navigating life under the influence of the culture and caretakers we're born into. These formative years shape our language, our tastes, our sense of self, and our place in the world.

I believe our instincts are not just our own but echoes of those who came before us.

But, might our *instincts*...

...keep us "safe" at first but eventually stifle us?

...give us a false sense of who we are?

...create patterns we don't even know we're repeating?

For example, imagine you're born with a naturally sensitive temperament (nature) your DNA has wired you to feel emotions deeply and pick up on subtle cues around you. If you grow up in a family that dismisses or ridicules emotional expression (nurture), you might internalize a belief that your feelings are "too much" or "wrong." Over time, that sensitivity, a gift by nature, gets paired with shame or suppression from nurture, forming an invisible bar in your cage: "I must hide my feelings to be accepted."

Or, you're born with a bold, adventurous temperament (nature), eager to try new things and take risks. But growing up, you're repeatedly told to "sit down," "don't be so loud," or punished for making mistakes (nurture). Eventually, you internalize the belief: "It's safer to stay small and invisible," dimming your natural spark. This becomes a bar: "I shouldn't take up space."

Maybe your DNA gifts you with a sharp, analytical mind (nature), and you love solving problems. But in your early environment, achievement is only celebrated if it looks a certain way, perhaps academic grades or athletic trophies, while your interests (e.g., art, tech, or unconventional paths) are dismissed (nurture). This creates the bar: "My dreams aren't valid unless they fit the mold."

What if you're naturally affectionate and relational (nature), thriving on connection. But you grow up in a family or culture where vulnerability is seen as weakness, or where love is withheld unless you "earn" it (nurture). This may build the bar: "I must prove my worth to deserve love," making intimacy feel like a transaction rather than a birthright.

3

Whether we're raised by a loving *"village"* or in isolation also shapes us profoundly. I was lucky. I spent summers on my grandparents' farm in Napa, California, painting barns, riding tractors, fixing fences. That land and those experiences left a permanent imprint.

Some people don't have memories of their grandparents at all. That contrast is powerful, and it shapes us, too.

Seeing the bars of our cage is only the beginning. Once we recognize how our nature and nurture have shaped the walls around us, we can start to notice something even more subtle: the rules we've agreed to live by inside that cage. These internal laws, often invisible, often unquestioned, dictate how far we believe we can go, what we believe we deserve, and who we believe we are. Some of these rules were written for us before we even knew how to speak. Others, we've etched ourselves without realizing. To truly free ourselves, we have to look at these rules, and decide which ones still belong.

Rules of the Cage

These internal rules emerge from both nature and nurture, written in us and around us until we learn to see and question them.

As we grow, we begin to form a kind of internal law, the confines of the cage, as it were. A personal code. Some of it we're aware of, but much of it is programming that lives in the subconscious. Don Miguel Ruiz cleverly presents this idea as "agreements," In his book *The Four Agreements*. This code tints the lens through which we see everything: our reactions, choices, values, and desires. Some parts are flexible, like pencil on paper. Others feel permanent, written in pen, or even etched in stone. Tipping my hat to you, Red Sox fans.

Only recently have many of us begun to realize that our internal codes could even be rewritten. But with the rise of therapy, coaching, and spiritual work, we've gained tools to examine and reframe these codes and subconscious patterns.

Pixar's *A Bug's Life* illustrates this adeptly. A colony of ants lives according to the status quo, until one brave soul challenges the system, inspires the community, and changes everything.

Unhealthy or outdated codes don't have to rule our lives. The more shadow work we do, the more capable we become of evaluating which parts of our script are still serving us, and which are not.

Shadow work simply means bringing what's hidden into the light, noticing the fears, habits, and beliefs we've tucked away because they felt too painful or unacceptable to face. It isn't about judgment or shame; it's about curiosity and compassion, learning to understand the parts of ourselves we've avoided so we can choose differently.

Here are some examples to illustrate how to bring something hidden to light through shadow work:

- *Journaling honestly about a moment you overreacted and asking yourself: "What was I really feeling underneath that?"*
- *Noticing when someone triggers you and instead of blaming them, asking: "What part of me feels threatened here?"*

- *Sitting quietly and naming the emotions you feel when you imagine failing at something, and tracing where you first learned to fear failure.*
- *Paying attention to repetitive patterns in relationships ("Why do I keep choosing unavailable partners?") and exploring what need or fear is driving it.*
- *Working with a therapist, coach, or trusted friend to say out loud the feelings or thoughts you've been afraid to admit to yourself.*

And yet, even as we examine the rules of the cage and begin rewriting the code, something remarkable happens, we notice that underneath it all, the bird has been singing the whole time.

Even within the cage, despite the bars and the old agreements, the song of who we truly are never stops. You may not have heard it clearly before, but it has been there, steady, quiet, waiting for you to listen.

Bird Song

Despite being in the cage, the bird still sings. Beneath the layers of conditioning and the weight of old codes, there is a quiet, unwavering melody, the truth of who you are, trying to be heard. Your emotions are that song. Sometimes they soar like a hymn of joy, and sometimes they cry out in sorrow or frustration, but they are always honest, always pointing you toward what's real.

A particular reading assignment when I was in high school has stuck with me all these years. "I Know Why the Caged Bird

Sings" by Maya Angelou, is a powerful reminder we all have a message, a story to share. And believe me when I say the many *layers* of irony are not lost on me.

For example, while I skimmed the book back then, I hadn't actually read it cover to cover. Yet here I am, writing a book, despite not having truly read one until my twenties; That I felt caged by my own silence, and hesitated to sing; that I read, er, uh, skimmed about the courage to speak up, yet it still took me years to find my own voice. *Layers.*

So how do we know which of these inner codes are actually serving us? That allows us access to sing our song?

Thankfully, we have an internal guidance system: our emotions. As Jerry and Esther Hicks teach in *"The Astonishing Power of Emotions,"* our emotions are not random, they're precise indicators of alignment, guiding us toward or away from our true path.

When we feel joy, ease, and enthusiasm, it signals that we are in harmony with our deeper self. When we feel anger, frustration, despair, or grief, those feelings are like a dashboard light blinking *check engine*, not to punish us, but to alert us that something needs our attention.

Challenging emotions are not inherently bad. As Shakespeare proclaimed, *"There is nothing good or bad, but thinking makes it so."* They're simply an alert to look closer.

Think of emotions like a fuel gauge. When the needle dips low, it's a signal to refuel. Ignore it, and you may find yourself stranded. Painful.

Pain, for example, can be a great motivator for change. But if it keeps you trapped or blocked, it's time to look deeper.

Access to your emotions is essential. If we can't access them, we can't name them. And if we can't name them, we can't truly understand them. Without understanding, we lose the ability to work with them skillfully, to let them guide us, teach us, or even release them when they no longer serve us.

That's why it's so important to gently address emotions that have been suppressed or repressed. Left unacknowledged, these emotions don't simply disappear; they often resurface in other ways, through our thoughts, behaviors, or even in our bodies as stress or illness.

By learning to access, name, and understand what we feel, we reclaim the ability to respond to life with clarity and authenticity rather than being unconsciously driven by hidden currents. Emotions, even the uncomfortable ones, are not enemies to conquer but messengers to hear, and when we listen, they can become powerful allies on the path to healing and growth.

But even as you listen to the internal song of your emotions and let them guide you, it's possible to misinterpret the melody, to confuse motion with progress, to flap your wings but go nowhere new. Sometimes the signals of pain or restlessness don't mean keep flying harder; they mean pause, look closer, and notice the pattern beneath you. If you're not careful, you may find yourself singing the same song, flying the same circle, mistaking familiar motion for true growth.

Flying in Circles

Not every flight takes you somewhere new. Sometimes, despite your best effort, you find yourself flapping the same wings, tracing the same sky, and landing right back where you began. At first, the movement feels like progress, but soon, the scenery becomes familiar, even tiresome. This is the quiet trap of flying in circles: mistaking motion for growth.

Another helpful indicator of where we are is the roundabout.

At 2:30am, a roundabout can feel like a blessing, no red lights, no delay. But if you find yourself circling endlessly, it may be a sign you're stuck in a pattern.

At first, the scenery seems new. Then you start to recognize it. Eventually you say, "*Wait!* I've been here before!"

As George Santayana reminds us, "*Those who can not remember the past are condemned to repeat it.*"

That's your cue: learn the lesson and exit the loop.

Here are some suggestions to help break free from the loop:

Pause and ask: "*What am I believing here that keeps me stuck?*", this question helps uncover the invisible story fueling the loop.

Make one small, deliberate change, even if it feels insignificant, like saying "*no*" where you always say "*yes,*" or choosing a different route home, to interrupt the pattern.

Write down the pattern as if you're observing someone else: "*This bird keeps doing X because...,*" creating distance helps you see it more clearly.

Ask yourself: *"What would my future self thank me for if I did differently right now?,"* this reframes the choice from fear to growth.

Experiment with doing the opposite of what you normally do in that situation, just to see what happens.

And yet, not every pattern is as simple to exit as veering out of the roundabout. Some loops run deeper, carved into us by pain, fear, or history, and they don't dissolve just because we finally see them. These are the patterns that feel less like circles in the sky and more like walls of stone: heavy, unyielding, and woven into our very sense of self. Breaking free from these requires more than noticing the loop, it asks us to face what we've been carrying and to believe that even the hardest stone can be reshaped.

When the Bars Turn to Stone

Some cages are easy to slip through once we see them. Others seem to dissolve the moment we question them. But then there are the bars that feel immovable, etched deep, heavy, unyielding. These are the ones forged in the fires of trauma, where experiences crystallize into beliefs so solid they feel like part of who we are. Solid stone. Yet even stone can be reshaped, softened, broken open.

If the stone you're carrying feels too heavy to loosen alone, that's not a failure, it's wisdom. Some bars are etched so deeply they ask for gentle, skilled support to help you see and soften them. Whether through therapy, somatic practices, energy healing, or simply speaking your truth to someone you trust, seeking help is not weakness, it's part of the path. Every bird needs a branch to rest on sometimes.

In the appendix, I'll share a technique I've found particularly effective for addressing difficult memories. For now, know that healing is possible, even for the deepest wounds.

Seeing the cage is the first step. The next is letting go of what no longer belongs to you.

Buda prompts us, *"In the end, only three things matter: how much you loved, how gently you lived, and how gracefully you let go of things not meant for you."*

Even the heaviest bars, the ones written in stone, hold spaces between them. Healing doesn't always mean shattering the entire cage at once, it begins with noticing the gaps, however narrow, where light and possibility still shine through. When the weight feels overwhelming, it helps to pause, to breathe, and to look more closely at what you're really holding onto, and what you can already begin to set down. The path forward starts in those quiet spaces, between the bars, where choice and freedom wait to be seen.

The Space Between the Bars

Sit quietly for a moment and bring to mind the invisible cage you've been living in, the walls built from what you inherited, what you were taught, and what you came to believe about yourself.

Ask yourself:
Which parts of this cage feel like they came from my nature?
Which parts feel like they came from my nurture?
Which bars of this cage no longer feel true?

Notice what comes up without judgment.

Remind yourself: seeing the cage is the beginning.

Whisper to yourself: *I am more than these bars. I can choose which ones to walk through and to leave behind.*

You've sat with the questions, felt the quiet truths, and begun to see the outlines of your cage and of yourself beyond it.

But recognizing the cage is not the same as leaving it.

To move forward, you must take what you've seen and turn it into choice. The cracks in the bars are waiting, but only you can decide to step through.

Exit Cage Left

You've seen the cage now, its bars, its patterns, its quiet hold on your wings. You've named where it came from, felt its weight, and glimpsed the spaces where light and freedom already wait. This awareness is your first act of flight, not yet soaring, but seeing.

But seeing is only the beginning.

To truly rise, you must also release.

The next step on your journey asks you to shed what no longer serves you, the stories, habits, and identities that feel safe but stifle your becoming. Just as a bird molts to grow new feathers, you, too, are invited to let go of the layers that no longer fit.

In the pages ahead, we'll explore how to meet this vulnerable, vital season with courage, discernment, and grace, and how each feather you release brings you closer to who you're meant to be.

Pre Flight:

Before you can soar, you must choose to step through the cracks you've seen.

- Witness the Cage - Gently notice the bars of nature, nurture, and habit that surround you.

- Listen to the Song Within - Hear what your emotions are telling you about which parts of your life feel true and which feel heavy.

- Move Toward the Gap - Begin to sing your own song as you step beyond the bars that once held you.

As you begin to shed what no longer serves you, you may feel lighter, clearer, even a little raw at first, like a bird in mid-molt, vulnerable but freer. You might notice more space to breathe, a quiet confidence returning, and glimpses of who you were always meant to be shining through. Every feather you release makes room for stronger, truer wings.

The sky is waiting, even if you start with one wing at a time.

SECTION 2: THE MOLTING SEASON

This sacred process of shedding lays the groundwork for what comes next, because the more we release, the more clearly we can see what was never ours to carry in the first place. Only by shedding what no longer fits can we rise into who we're becoming. This section invites you into the vulnerable but vital season of molting, letting go of old stories, habits, and beliefs so you can step into who you are becoming. Here you'll learn how to question what you've been handed, discern what belongs to you, and make conscious choices about what to carry forward and what to leave behind.

The First Feather Falls

Once we've seen how the cage was built, from the stories of our ancestors, the words of our caretakers, and the patterns we inherited, we can begin to molt.

Molting is messy, vulnerable, and necessary. To molt is the natural process of shedding what no longer serves you, old patterns, beliefs, or layers, to make space for growth and renewal.

This sacred process of shedding is important even when it feels familiar and comfortable, even when it feels like part of who you are.

We carry the stories of our ancestors in our blood, predispositions and patterns written into our being before we even arrive.

I'll never forget a time I realized a story I carried wasn't truly mine. I was out mending a fence with my grandfather, trying to pry a wire into place. I remember him growing impatient, grabbing the pliers out of my hands, and finishing the task himself. In that moment, I absorbed his impatience as a reflection of my own inadequacy, a quiet, persistent belief that I had to be perfect to be worthy. Years later, I would see it clearly for what it was: his impatience was not my essence. And with that realization, I felt the first feather fall.

Who we become is profoundly shaped by the hands that held us, the words that reached us, the lessons we learned, and sometimes, the ones we learned too soon.

I remember being about ten when it struck me: it's not nature versus nurture.

It's both.
Always both.

We are what we're born with, what we've lived through, and what we choose to do with both.

Why Shedding Sets You Free

To know yourself means to embrace both parts of the equation.

To honor the gifts and challenges of your nature, to look at your ancestry, your constitution, your temperament, even the cosmic map you were born under, without judgment.

And to honestly examine your nurture, your story, your past, the things you learned to believe about yourself and the world, with compassion.

We can't change our genes. We can't rewrite our childhood. But we can choose what to do with them now.

Self-knowledge isn't about arriving at some final answer. It's about standing inside the infinite mystery, and choosing to understand the one thing that's yours to understand: you.

Once we start noticing what we're carrying, and what no longer serves, we also start noticing what others try to hand us. Often, what they offer comes wrapped in words: opinions, judgments, stories, instructions. Learning how to receive, or not receive, those words is part of the molt too.

To shed what no longer serves, we first have to see it clearly, and that begins with the questions we dare to ask ourselves.

Molting Through Questions

Charles Kettering said, *"A problem well stated is a problem half solved."*
Which is great, if you can even define the problem in the first place.

But what if you can't?

That's where questions come in.
I've learned (and often remind my clients) that *"The power of the answer, depends on the quality of the question."*

The caliber of the question is what allows you to even see, and state, the problem clearly.

Being mindful of the questions you pose to yourself is part of being conscious.
If you walk through life subconsciously, or even consciously, asking:
Why does this always happen to me?
You've already framed the answer into a corner.
That question assumes inevitability, assumes helplessness.
It subtly invites answers that keep you stuck.

But if instead you ask:
What can I do so this no longer happens to me?
You open an entirely different door.
That question assumes possibility, assumes agency.
It invites you to look for choices, to take action, to evolve.

The answers to those two questions could mean the difference between living an intentional life and being subjected to one.

It's also important to phrase your questions from a place of belief that you *will* have access to a meaningful, usable answer.

Questions that come from despair tend to lead you deeper into despair.
Questions that come from faith in yourself, even shaky faith, tend to guide you toward light.

On the following page are a few examples of how to reframe your questions:

Do you feel a difference in the energy of the phrasing?

Instead of asking...	**Try asking...**
Why does nothing ever work out for me?	*What would it take for this to work out?*
Why can't I catch a break?	*What can I change to create a breakthrough?*
Why am I like this?	*What part of me is asking to grow right now?*
What's wrong with me?	*What's the next step I can take to feel more aligned?*
Why does everyone else have it figured out but me?	*What can I learn from others that will help me take my next step?*

One line of questioning keeps you tethered to your cage. The other invites you to molt, to climb, to fly.

So when you catch yourself in a spiral of unhelpful questions, pause.
And ask:
Is this question worthy of the answer I'm seeking?

Because the question you ask sets the direction of the answer you receive.

As we become more conscious of the questions we're asking ourselves, and the answers we're willing to receive, we also become more aware of the words, ideas, and energy that others throw our way. Not every question deserves an answer, and not every idea needs to be caught and held.

Invitation to action:

Write down one belief you're ready to shed.

Take one action to release it (journal, have a conversation, set a boundary).
Celebrate even the smallest act of letting go.

Just as we can choose the quality of the questions we pose to ourselves, we can also choose what to catch, and what to let fall.

Preening Our Feathers

Words, whether spoken or written, carry with them the intentions of the person who sends them. There are a few things worth keeping in mind when we engage in these words offered by others, past or present.

Words are only representations of the reality they're meant to convey.
But words are not reality.
They're symbols, placeholders. At best, they're maps of a territory we may never fully see the same way. They're arrows pointing toward something, not the thing itself.

And just like a map can lead you to beautiful or barren places, so too can words. Before you follow where they point, pause to decide which destinations are truly yours to visit, and which are better left unexplored.

Preening our feathers is the daily act of tending to what we choose to carry. Just as a bird smooths, cleans, and discards what no longer serves the integrity of its wings, so too must we sort through the words, stories, and beliefs that land on us. Some strengthen our plumage, adding luster and lift; others weigh us down, matted and out of place. By mindfully grooming the feathers we accept and letting the rest fall away, we preserve not only our ability to fly, but the grace and strength with which we take to the skies.

Ask yourself:
"What is the feather they're really offering?"
"And do I even want to keep it?"

Take a quiet moment with your journal. Recall a recent word, comment, or story someone offered you, maybe praise, maybe criticism, maybe just casual advice. Imagine it as a single feather placed in your hand. Hold it up to your heart and ask: *Does this feather strengthen my wings, or does it weigh me down?* Write about what it feels like to accept it into your plumage, or what it feels like to release it to the wind. As you do this with different words and memories, notice the patterns that emerge. *Which kinds of feathers truly help you soar? Which ones keep you tethered?* Over time, you'll begin to recognize which feathers belong in your flight, and which are better left behind.

Feathers To Keep

These are the words, beliefs, and lessons that truly nourish your flight, light, strong, and aligned with who you are becoming:

- The encouragement from a teacher who believed in your potential when you couldn't yet see it.

- The kindness of a stranger that showed you how small gestures can change someone's day.

- A family value of resilience, the knowledge that you can rise after falling.

- A memory of joy, laughter, or connection that reminds you what matters most.

- Wisdom that invites you to grow without shaming where you are.

These feathers feel warm in your hand, like they belong,

strengthening your wings instead of weighing them down.

Feathers to Clip

These are the words, beliefs, and stories that no longer fit, heavy, brittle, or tangled in someone else's pain:

- "You'll never be good enough."

- "People like us don't do things like that."

- Conditional love that required you to shrink, silence, or disguise who you truly are.

- The shame from a single mistake replayed louder than all your successes combined.

- Comparisons that convinced you you had to compete just to deserve belonging.

These feathers feel sharp or sticky, clinging but uncomfortable, and they lose their grip the moment you choose to release them.

Because some feathers are worth treasuring.
And some are better left to drift away. We get to choose.

This practice of noticing which feathers to keep and which to release doesn't end here, it continues in how you listen, how you clarify what is truly being offered, and how you choose what belongs in your wings. The next exercises will help you deepen that discernment.

So, when someone speaks, or when you read, take care.

Don't just listen to respond.

Listen to understand.

Holding space and truly hearing someone when they share their message, and express their voice can be powerful and liberating. Validation for both parties.

When we truly hold space for someone, and for ourselves, to express what's inside, it's not just liberating, it's illuminating. It can show us what feels authentic and what feels heavy, what aligns with our truth and what does not.

When we engage with the words of another, whether spoken, written, or even implied, it's easy to believe we understand them just because we recognize the words they use. But words are slippery; they carry personal histories, unspoken contexts, and subtle shades of meaning that can differ wildly between speaker and listener.

If we want to truly listen, not just to the sound of the words, but to the heart of what is being offered, we must slow down. We must be willing to notice what we assume, to question what we've decided too quickly, and to leave space for clarification and choice.

With that in mind, here is a simple, two-part practice to help you discern what is being offered and whether it belongs with you.

First: The fluffy red feather exercise.

We all know what "*fluffy*" means. We know what "*red*" means. We know what "*feather*" means.

But just because we all know the words doesn't mean we're imagining the same fluffy red feather.

The author or speaker has a specific feather in mind, maybe a cardinal's plume, maybe a carnival boa, maybe a downy craft feather from childhood.
And if we assume we've grasped their exact meaning without checking, we may completely miss what they were actually offering.

Part of listening, truly listening, is learning to uncover what the author actually intends.
We do this through reflective listening, by asking questions, by clarifying:
"Is this what you mean?"
"Can you describe your feather to me?"

Second: you don't have to catch the feather at all.
If someone offers you a feather that's tattered, heavy with someone else's pain, or simply doesn't belong in your quill, you're not obligated to keep it.

You can simply let it drift to the ground.
You are free to examine it if you choose, or to walk away.

Paraphrasing Aristotle: *It is the mark of an educated mind to consider an idea without accepting it.*

When we learn which *"feathers"* to tuck into our wings and which to release, which stories to keep and which to let go, something else begins to emerge: space.

The more we discern what belongs to us and what does not, the more room we create between stimulus and response.

And in that space, a quiet stillness waits, an awareness deeper than words, beneath the noise of reaction.

It is in this stillness, between the layers of body, heart, and spirit, where we begin to truly hear ourselves.

The Stillness Between Layers

Before a bird can take flight, it must first feel the air, not just the gusts that lift it, but the subtle currents that swirl around and within it.

You are no different.

We often rush through life, flapping and striving, without ever noticing the quiet spaces where the real work happens. But just as the bird senses the wind before it leaps, you too are invited to pause and feel the invisible forces shaping you.

It is in this stillness, between what has happened and how you respond, that you discover the layers of your being.

This is where we begin.

Part of raising our consciousness is simply learning to observe. Not to fix, not to analyze, not to judge, just to notice.

It sounds simple enough. But there are layers to observation, and each one requires its own kind of awareness.

We begin by observing how we feel *physically*.
What is our body saying? Are our shoulders tight? Is our breath shallow? Are our hands restless, or calm?
Then we observe how we feel *emotionally*.
What stories are running in the background? Is there anger

under the surface? Sadness? Gratitude? What does our heart feel, beneath the noise?

And then we observe how we feel *spiritually*.
This one can be the hardest to put into words. Is there a sense of connection or disconnection? Do you feel open or closed? Do you feel aligned with something greater, or far from it? Each of these, body, heart, spirit, asks for a distinct kind of listening.

Practice: The Three Layers of Observation

Preparation:

Find a quiet space where you won't be disturbed. Sit or lie down comfortably. Take a few slow, deep breaths to settle. Keep a journal or notebook nearby to record your insights if you wish. Let your shoulders drop. Let your jaw soften. Let your mind settle.

Step 1: Listening to the Body

- Close your eyes and bring your attention to your physical body.

- Scan yourself slowly from head to toe.

  - Notice your shoulders: are they tight or relaxed?

  - Feel your breath: is it shallow, deep, fast, slow?

  - Observe your hands: are they fidgeting, calm, tense?

○ Check your stomach, jaw, neck, anywhere that feels alive or heavy.

Without trying to change anything, simply name what you feel: tightness, warmth, tingling, heaviness, ease...

Journal Prompt:

What is my body telling me right now? Where does it feel open? Where does it feel closed?

Step 2: Listening to the Heart

- Shift your focus inward to your emotional landscape.

- What feelings are present beneath the surface?

    ○ Is there anger simmering? Sadness waiting?

    ○ Is there joy, gratitude, curiosity?

    ○ What stories or memories are quietly playing in the background?

- Let yourself feel without judgment, simply notice what arises.

Journal Prompt:

What is my heart feeling right now? What emotions are alive, and what are they trying to tell me?

Step 3: Listening to the Spirit

- Now, tune into your sense of connection, to yourself, others, the world, or something greater.

- Does your spirit feel open or closed?

- Do you feel aligned or out of step with your values and purpose?

- Is there a sense of connection, peace, or disconnection and longing?

This may not come in words, it may feel like a color, a sensation, an image, or simply a knowing.

Journal Prompt:

What is my spirit whispering to me right now? Do I feel connected or separate? Open or guarded?

Close it out:

Now pause and notice:
How have today's outside circumstances, a conversation, a task, the weather, touched each of these layers?

Take one more deep breath and thank yourself for showing up to listen. Notice if anything has shifted, even slightly, simply because you paused to observe.

When ready, gently open your eyes and, if you like, write down a few words or intentions to carry forward:

What does my body need? What does my heart need? What does my spirit need?

And as we practice detached observing, we also begin to notice something else: how *outside circumstances* affect each of these layers.

A sharp word from a stranger tightens the chest.
A sudden kindness softens the heart.
A stormy sky stirs something ancient in the spirit.

If we move too quickly, we miss the chance to see what's happening.
We react on autopilot.
We clench, withdraw, explode, without understanding why.

But as Viktor E. Frankl reminds us:
"Between stimulus and response there is a space.
In that space is our power to choose our response.
In our response lies our growth and our freedom."

That space is everything.

Observation gives us the space.
The space gives us the choice.
And the choice gives us the freedom to evolve.

So we keep practicing:
Watching.
Noticing.
Breathing into that space between what happens *to* us and what happens *through* us.

In that space, we can find ourselves.

This way of listening doesn't have to stay confined to quiet moments on a cushion, it can travel with you into your daily life. As you move through your day, pause whenever you can to check in: What is my body saying as I stand in line? What is my heart feeling in this conversation? What is my spirit whispering as I face this choice? Am I okay with how I responded to that person? To that situation?

These small moments of awareness, amid the noise of errands, meetings, and routines, help you stay attuned to yourself even when the winds pick up around you. In time, this gentle noticing becomes a kind of compass, guiding you toward choices and actions that honor all of who you are. Let your body, heart, and spirit speak, not just in stillness, but in the living rhythm of your everyday.

As you sit in that stillness, between body, heart, and spirit, you begin to realize something profound: stillness is not the destination.

It is the vantage point.

From here, you can feel the wind more clearly. You can sense which currents are yours to ride and which are simply passing through.

And when the noise quiets and the layers settle, you begin to see the truth: every choice you make is a wingbeat. Every thought, every step, every yes or no is shaping the path ahead.

The stillness teaches you to notice.

But choosing, that's what gives you flight.

So now, from this quiet awareness, you're ready to take the next step: choosing your flight path.

Plotting Your Trajectory

By now, you've begun to see yourself more clearly, the cage you've lived in, the feathers you've shed, and the song that has always been yours.

This self-awareness brings with it a gift, and a responsibility.

The gift is clarity: you can see, perhaps for the first time, that you have choices.
The responsibility is action: to choose wisely what comes next.

You still have to decide which direction to fly, what to release, what to carry, and where you truly want to go.

Because awareness alone doesn't carry you forward. It's time to start choosing your trajectory, consciously, courageously, and in alignment with the person you're becoming.

Life is full of air currents, each one carrying you along a different path.
Every day, dozens of them swirl around you, opportunities, relationships, habits, conversations, thoughts, each one offering to lift you somewhere.

If we're not paying attention, we might catch the first current that comes along, one that is just distraction, or one we're expected or obligated to take, without even noticing where it's headed. We settle into it, let it carry us, and then wonder why we feel lost or frustrated when the view below looks nothing like where we intended to go.

But if we're conscious, if we pause and actually sense which way the wind is blowing, we can choose if it truly serves us.

But even when we *can* see the currents and *could* choose, many of us hesitate, not because we don't know what we want, but because we quietly question whether we're worthy of it. Whether we're allowed to divert off the expected path, to claim a wind that feels truer to us, even if no one else understands it. We forget that permission is not something granted by others, it's something we give ourselves. The sky has always been open to you; the question is whether you're willing to trust your wings enough to chart your own course.

And if you decided you wanted to glide from Point A to Point Z, you wouldn't knowingly ride a current blowing you in the opposite direction. And yet that's exactly what we do when we pick up habits, jobs, relationships, or beliefs that don't actually take us where we say we want to go.

For example:
If your goal is peace of mind, but you keep letting yourself get swept into the storm of gossip and conflict, don't be surprised when you find yourself far from peaceful.

If your goal is financial independence, but you keep riding the gusts of impulse spending and procrastination, you'll just keep circling the same patch of sky indefinitely.

If your goal is meaningful connection, but you drift with those who belittle your dreams and pull you toward bitterness, you may land somewhere you never wanted to be.

And here's the thing: it's not just about which current you catch, it's also about who's riding that wind with you.

Sometimes the birds around you are heading to a completely different destination. And if you're not paying attention, they may pressure you to dive too soon or deviate off course into skies that were never yours to fly.

So ask yourself:
Where do I say I want to go?

Is this current, this thought, this choice, this relationship, actually carrying me there?

Are the ones flying with me moving in the same direction, or are they pulling me off course?

And maybe most importantly: how long are you willing to ride a wind that's taking you farther and farther from where you truly want to land?

Because the longer you let yourself be carried past the point of alignment, the more it costs you, in time, in energy, and in whatever you've already invested to get there.

The beauty of life is that there's always another current. If you realize you're riding the wrong one, you can always shift, wait, and catch the one that truly carries you toward where you're meant to go.

The more we shed what no longer serves us and learn to ask better questions, the more clearly we begin to see the choices before us, and the more responsibility we have to choose wisely.

After all, every choice is like catching a current of wind. And we know not every current is carrying you where you truly want to go.

So pay attention. The current you choose matters. The sooner you notice where you are, and where you're really trying to go, the easier it becomes to slip out of what doesn't serve and wait for the wind that does.

But choosing your current is only half of it. Every path, no matter how open the sky may seem, has its own immovable fixtures: the rooted trees, the fixed pipes, the obstacles you can't simply wish away.

One of the most valuable lessons I learned while plumbing swimming pool equipment was this: first, figure out which ends of the pipe are fixed, the points you *can't* move. Then, calculate the path between them and plumb accordingly.

Creating a flightplan is much the same. You can't move a tree that's rooted in the middle of your path. If you're looking for a place to land, rest, or preen, the first step is to identify the immovable pieces, the fixed realities you'll have to work around, and then adjust your plans with those in mind.

Knowing what can and cannot be moved gives you clarity, saves you wasted effort, and helps you design a path that actually works.

Once you've honored what's fixed, you're free to navigate the open sky between, with intention, grace, and room to soar.

So what are the fixed points in your life right now? And where can you adjust your flight path to meet them with ease?

Every choice you make, every time you pause to consider whether this path, this habit, this relationship is truly aligned, you're strengthening your wings.

And when you've shed enough, when you've chosen enough, when you've finally molted the weight that kept you circling, something shifts.

When the molting is done, you're not just lighter, you're ready. Ready to step into the next season of your becoming.

When the Molting is Done

After all, choosing your flight path isn't just about picking the next draft or adjusting around the trees you can't move, it's also about claiming the wings you've been strengthening all along.

Each choice you've made, to shed old stories, to set down the stones you've carried, to ask better questions and honor your truth, has been part of your molting.

And when you've done the work of shedding what no longer belongs to you, and you stand lighter, clearer, and more aligned... that's when the next season arrives.

As you shed what no longer belongs to you, you may feel raw, exposed, or uncertain. That's okay. That's natural. The shell of who you thought you had to be will feel tight and fragile just before it breaks.

If what you're shedding feels too heavy to carry alone, that's okay, you don't have to do this by yourself. Reach out for help when you need it.

Trust that what falls away was never meant to be permanent. Trust that what remains is closer to your truth, stronger, clearer, more aligned.

Place your hands over your heart and ask yourself:
What am I ready to let go of?
What part of me is emerging underneath?
How can I honor this vulnerable, beautiful version of me right now?

And as you perch here, between what was and what will be,

remember: each layer you shed, each truth you claim, each step of accountability you take fortifies you. You are not breaking down. You are breaking through.

You do not have to rush this. You do not have to finish all at once.
Let yourself rest in the knowing that you are already becoming. Becoming stronger.

If it feels heavy, false, forced, or out of alignment, it might not belong to you anymore.

You've released what no longer serves you, the stones, the old stories, the worn-out feathers. e.g., *"I must always be the strong one," "My worth depends on my productivity," staying in friendships that drain me, saying yes when I mean no...etc.* You've felt the lightness that comes with letting go, and you've glimpsed the space that's been waiting for you all along.

But before you leap into what's next, you need a place to gather yourself, to weave together the pieces of who you are becoming.

Every bird returns to the nest, not just to rest, but to remember.

Here, you pause. You reflect. You gather the twigs and feathers of your nature and nurture, and you begin to weave them into something strong enough to hold you, and flexible enough to grow with you.

This next section is your nest.
A place to sit with your story.

To feel your roots.
To envision your flight.

When you're ready, the sky will still be there.
But for now, let's begin here, in the quiet of the nest.

How does shedding lead to gathering what remains and weaving it into a stronger foundation?

Before you soar, you return to the nest, not to retreat, but to weave together the feathers of who you've become into a foundation strong enough to support your next flight.

SECTION 3: NEST, FEATHERS, AND THE FLOCK

Part 1: Navigating the Branches, Where You Are and Where You're Going

You've already seen how nature and nurture can create the invisible cage that confines you. But those same forces, your roots, your experiences, your connections, also create the tree that holds you steady and the nest that shelters you. Where the cage limits, the tree supports. Where the cage feels like obligation, the flock offers belonging.

The Tree That Holds You

Your nest does not float in midair.
It is held, cradled, and supported by something much larger, a tree that has been growing quietly beneath and around you your entire life.

The roots of this tree reach deep into the soil of where you came from, your ancestry, your temperament, your nature.

Its trunk grows sturdy through the seasons of your experience, shaped by the people, places, and moments that have nurtured (and sometimes tested) you. And its branches stretch outward and upward, reaching toward what you are becoming, toward the sky that still waits for you.

The nest, your present moment, your safe space of self-knowing, rests in the crook of this tree, supported by all that you've been given, all that you've lived, and all that you are growing into.

When you see only the nest, it's easy to forget what's holding you up.
But when you pause to see the whole tree, roots, trunk, branches, you begin to understand how deeply supported you already are, and how much possibility still lies ahead.

So before you take the next step, let's step back and honor your tree.
Map it out. See it whole. Remember what anchors you, what holds you steady, and what calls you higher.

Exercise: Roots and Branches

Take a quiet moment with pencil and paper, or, if you're feeling ambitious, a chisel and stone.

Draw a tree, roots below, trunk in the middle, branches above.

- In the roots, write what you feel came from your nature: your ancestry, your temperament, your birth chart.
- In the trunk, write what came from your nurture: the people, experiences, and environments that shaped

you.

- In the branches, write what you're choosing to grow into now, the qualities and directions you're cultivating.

When you finish, take in the whole tree. That's you, roots, trunk, and branches.

Now, circle one insight from your tree or feathers that feels alive for you, and write one small, concrete action you can take this week to honor it.

Journal Prompt

After completing the tree, reflect:
What of me was given to me?
What of me was taught to me?
And who am I choosing to become now?

Write without editing. Let the answers surprise you.

Branching Out

The nest gives you safety, but the branches offer direction. They stretch out before you like choices on a map, each one leading somewhere new.

This is where self-reflection meets movement, where clarity becomes action. To fly forward, you must also learn to navigate the branches, to choose with intention which path will carry you toward your becoming.

Knowing yourself also means knowing where the destination lies from where you are. As Stephen Covey invites you to:

"Begin with the end in mind."

Martin Luther King, Jr. adds, *"While it is important to know your destination for context, "You don't have to see the whole staircase, just take the first step."*

Lao Tzu Chimes in:
"A journey of a thousand miles begins with a single step."
So which step is most important?
The next one.

Even though you cannot see them all from where you stand.

Then it's like planning a road trip:
The gear you pack depends on the journey and destination ahead. Your mode of travel is equally important in planning. Are you walking? Driving?... Flying?? (*Ha!*)

I believe navigating the blocks and obstacles between ourselves and our truth is a worthy journey. It lets us access our power, evolve to our highest potential, and share our voice from a place of clarity.

Questions to Navigate Your Branches

- Where am I on my journey right now, emotionally, spiritually, mentally, and physically?
- What does "the end in mind" look or feel like for me? If nothing were impossible, what would my destination be?
- What kind of journey am I currently on: am I walking, driving, flying, and what does that metaphor mean to me?

- What "gear" (skills, resources, support) do I already carry that could help me move forward?
- What obstacles have I encountered that feel like blockages between me and my truth?
- How have I already evolved through past obstacles, and what did I learn from them?
- What voices (mine or others') might be influencing where I think I should go, and are they aligned with what I truly want?
- What's one choice I've been avoiding, and what would happen if I took just one small step toward it?
- Who or what inspires me when I feel lost or uncertain about my path?
- If my journey were a story or a map, what chapter or marker am I standing at now, and what might the next chapter hold?

Beyond the Branch

The tree is not your enemy. It is not your cage. The tree is a gift.

It stands steady through seasons and storms, offering you a place to land when your wings are tired, a vantage point from which to see the terrain ahead, and branches that cradle you when you need rest, renewal, or courage to climb higher.

And it's more than a tree. It is also the embodiment of the mentors, ancestors, and loved ones who came before you, rooting deep into the earth, holding space for your becoming, and reminding you in their quiet strength: *"You are held. You are safe. You can climb higher when you're ready."*

But the tree is not your destination.

If you cling too long to its safety, the branches that once supported you can begin to feel like shackles. When the wind comes, as it always does, you may find yourself gripping tighter, immobilized by your own comfort.

You were never meant to live your life nestled on a single branch.

The wind is not your enemy either. It comes to test you, to strengthen your wings, to awaken your belief that you can fly.

Confidence is not born from sitting still. It is born from leaping, again and again, until your wings learn how to catch you.

So use the tree for what it is: a sacred resting place, a teacher in stillness. But do not confuse it for the sky.

The moment comes when you must loosen your grip on the familiar and leap, not because you feel fully ready, but because you've grown too large to stay.

And when you finally let go, when you trust the wind to carry you beyond the safety of the branch, you begin to notice something else.

The air catches you not just because of your wings, but because of what you bring into it.

You realize that every leap, every glide, every return to the tree has colored your feathers, shaped the way you shine, the way you're seen, the way you see yourself.

If the tree gave you roots and the wind gives you lift, it's your feathers that tell your story.

So before you climb higher, pause and notice: what colors are you already carrying into the sky?

Part 2: The Colors of Your Feathers

Every bird's plumage is unique, a living record of where it has been, what it has endured, and who it is becoming. Each feather holds a story: some bold and brilliant, others soft and subtle, but all of them part of the whole.

You, too, carry your story in the colors of your feathers, in the way you speak, move, love, stumble, and rise again.

Some of these colors you chose.
Some were given to you before you even knew how to choose. And some you are still discovering, shimmering just beneath the surface, waiting for light.

What moments in your life brought out your brightest colors? What patterns or traits feel like they were painted on you by others? Which colors feel like they're yours alone? Which still seem hidden, waiting to be revealed?

The more clearly you see the colors you carry, the more confidently you can bring your full self into the world, letting your unique plumage guide you toward the skies meant for you.

Remember: every color, whether chosen, inherited, or discovered, has shaped who you are. You're allowed to keep, deepen, soften, or even let go of the shades that no longer serve you, the choice is yours.

And yet, even as you choose and shape your colors, it's important to remember: you don't have to know everything about yourself, or about life, all at once. Part of the beauty of your plumage lies in its mystery. Some feathers reveal themselves only over time, and some you may never fully understand. That's okay. The point isn't to know it all, but to know yourself enough to keep becoming.

If information is infinite, we can never know it all, and honestly, who would want to? Imagine a life with nothing left to discover, no mystery to marvel at, no questions left to ask.

We don't even need to understand everything about the things we use and depend on every day in order to function and thrive, and that's okay.

For example: how many drivers know the exact ignition timing of their car's engine, down to the degree before top dead center? (Homage to Marisa Tomei.)

A vanishingly small number.
And yet, more than 1.6 billion vehicles make their way down the road just fine.

So if we don't have to know everything about everything, where should we focus our curiosity?

Socrates reminds us: *"Know thyself."*
Plato adds: *"The first and greatest victory is to conquer yourself."*

And what does it mean to truly know yourself? It means not just seeing your colors, but taking responsibility for them, for the choices you've made, for the patterns you've carried, and for the way you show up in the world. Self-knowledge without accountability is like admiring your plumage in the mirror but neglecting to tend to it. Part of accepting who you are, and who you are becoming, is accepting accountability.

This acknowledgment not only creates outward ripples, shaping how you're experienced by others, but it also protects your inner integrity. You take inventory of decisions you've made, and you nest in it. Accountability fortifies your character, anchoring you in honesty and self-respect.

One way to further your knowing is to pause and examine the colors of your own feathers, to see what you carry, explore what you've chosen, and what still waits to be claimed.

Suggested Exercise: Feather Inventory

Sit somewhere quiet with a journal and a handful of colorful markers or pencils.
On a blank page, draw a simple outline of a wing or a cluster of feathers.
On each feather, write a word, phrase, or memory that feels like part of you, a trait, a value, a challenge you've overcome, a gift you carry, a dream you still hold.

- What feathers do you notice most?
- Which ones feel fully yours?
- Which ones feel inherited?
- Which ones are still waiting for you to claim them?

Suggested Visualization: The Feather and the Wind

Close your eyes and imagine standing in an open field, holding a single feather, one of yours.

Notice its color, texture, weight. Feel how it quivers in the wind.
Now lift it high and let it go, watch it dance and swirl, carried by the breeze.
As it floats, ask yourself:

- Where has this feather already flown?
- What story does it carry?
- Where is the wind inviting it (and you) to go next?

When you're ready, open your eyes and write down what came to you.

Journal Prompts

- Which of my "feathers" have I been most proud of? Why?
- Which feather feels hardest to accept, and what would it mean to honor it anyway?
- What colors in me have I inherited, and what colors have I chosen?
- What new feathers do I want to grow this year?
- If my life so far could be described as a single, magnificent feather, what would it look like?

Remember: the colors of your feathers are not fixed. They deepen, soften, shift with the seasons.
Some may molt and fall away, making room for new growth.

All are worthy. All belong.

And if you ever forget what you're made of, come back to
your feathers, and to the tree that holds you.
Because every bird, every soul, carries a story worth seeing,
one plume at a time.

Part 3: Birds of a Feather

Who to Share Your Nest With

Once you've begun to navigate your own branches and notice the colors of your feathers, another choice presents itself: who will you bring into the sky with you?

Not everyone you've met on the journey deserves to sit in the heart of your nest. Not everyone can honor the sanctuary you've created.
And that's not a judgment, it's wisdom.

So before you fly too far, pause.
Look around.
And ask yourself who truly belongs beside you, and who is better left on the branch, the porch, I mean... perch... or the horizon.

It's okay that not everyone is meant to sit in your nest.

You're not everyone's cup of tea, some people prefer coffee. Others aren't even thirsty.

You don't have to share your nest just because someone happens to be nearby.

Proximity is not permission.

You don't owe everyone access to your nest. There's a very different energy when you do something out of love versus out of obligation. You can care for someone, even have a deep affinity for them, and still love them from a distance.

So how do you know who belongs in your inner circle?

The key is **discernment**.

Ask yourself:
How do I feel when I'm flying in formation with this person?
When I grow tired, can they step up and share the draft, or do they leave me flapping alone?
When it's their turn to lead, can I follow with trust?
After spending time with them, do I feel lighter and energized, or heavy and drained?
Do they honor my boundaries? Do I honor theirs?

Not everyone deserves equal access to your energy, and not everyone needs to be invited all the way in.

Some belong at the heart of your nest.
Others may belong on the outer branches.
And some? They're perfectly fine staying out on the perch.

Your space is sacred.
Treat it that way, with care, discernment, and love for yourself and for those who truly deserve to share its warmth.

Another sacred area where discernment matters just as much is in choosing your sources of information.

Be just as selective with what, and who, you allow to speak into your mind as you are with who you let sit in your nest. Not every voice deserves your attention. Not every opinion deserves your consideration. Accept that people do things for their reasons, not ours.

And remember: *Eagles don't concern themselves with what pigeons have to say.*

When you're choosing what to believe and where to place your trust, ask yourself the same questions you'd ask about your flock: Does this voice uplift or diminish me? Does it help me see clearly or cloud my vision? Does it align with the kind of bird I aspire to become?

Boundaries are healthy, in relationships and in the information you consume.
It's okay if saying no feels hard at first.

Every time you choose your own peace, you make space for those who truly honor your flight, and for the kind of wisdom that helps you soar higher.

Feather in Your Cap

Once you've traced your roots, walked your branches, chosen your feathers, and gathered your flock, you may begin to notice something stirring inside you, a quiet readiness, a subtle hum beneath the surface, as if the air itself has started to move in your favor.

You've built your nest with care, discerned what to carry and who to carry it with.
You've honored your roots, claimed your colors, and chosen your companions wisely.
And now, the wind calls you beyond the branches.
It invites you to trust the invisible currents, to lift your wings, and to meet whatever waits beyond the safety of what you've known.

Because no matter how sturdy and sacred your nest may be, you were never meant to stay there forever.

And when you know your roots, you stand more steady and sure, no matter how the winds may shift.

This clarity, of where you come from, who you are, and who flies beside you, becomes the quiet confidence that carries you when the sky grows wide and wild.

When the air begins to stir and the branches sway, that is your moment, to rise, to feel the wind against your feathers, and to discover what it truly means to ride the currents of your own becoming.

So put this feather in your cap, a mark of where you've been and a promise of where you're going.

Then, when you're ready, let's step into the next season, where the wind becomes your teacher, and the sky, your path.

SECTION 4: THE WIND

The wind has a way of humbling even the most confident wings.

You feel it before you see it, brushing your feathers, lifting you when you least expect it, changing direction just as you think you've found your course.

Some days it carries you higher than you ever imagined; other days it tests you, stripping away what you thought you needed so you can finally feel its true power beneath you.

But the wind is not just something outside of you. It is also within you, a force that whispers, *move, stretch, rise.*

The wind reminds us that our lives are not meant to stay still. It asks something of us: to pay attention, to respond, to move with it rather than against it.

And yet, before we can ride the wind, we must understand what moves us, what gives shape to our flight and purpose to our journey.

Which brings us here: to the sequence that lifts us from the nest and carries us into the currents.

The Sequence of Flight

Socrates posed, *"The unexamined life is not worth living."*

But what is there to examine? Just our thoughts?

I suspect there's a reason we have been given the ability to live beyond the confines of a brain in a jar on a shelf.

We have wings. And talons.
We were not meant to spend our entire lives in the nest.

Josiah Gilbert Holland reminds us: *"God gives every bird its food, but he does not throw it into the nest."*

We were meant for flight.
Destined to *soar*.

And when fear keeps us perched too long?

W. Clement Stone offers: *"Thinking will not overcome fear but action will."*

Considering we are here for just a wisp of wind, a brief, breathtaking moment in the sky, it stands to reason that action is paramount.

But what shapes our actions?
Intentions.

Which begs the deeper question: what prompts our intentions?

Dr. Wayne W. Dyer invites us to see intention as more than mere resolve. In *The Power of Intention*, he describes it as a force in the universe itself, a creative, energetic current that allows the act of creation to take place. Intention is how we connect and co-create with the wind that carries us.

So how do we arrive at intention?

We begin by fixing our attention, as Napoleon Hill so powerfully exhorts, on *desire*. As he emphatically states:

> *"The starting point of all achievement is desire."*

But the type of desire matters. I'm not talking about the kind that is rooted in greed, lust, or the empty pursuit of more for its own sake.

The kind of desire worth cultivating is the one that calls something into your life because you believe it will deepen you, something that aligns with the core of who you truly are, and guides you toward becoming the best version of yourself.

This is the desire that doesn't just chase what glitters, but seeks what grounds, strengthens and helps you grow and evolve into someone you're proud to be.

And so the sequence emerges:

Desire → Intention → Action → Result → Reflection → Evolution.

This process is less a straight ladder and more a spiral, each turn bringing us back to the beginning but from a higher vantage point. Desire re-emerges, not as the same longing that once stirred us, but as a refined echo shaped by what we've learned. Intention sharpens with new wisdom, action becomes more aligned, results arrive with greater clarity, and reflection reveals subtler truths. Evolution, then, is not an endpoint but a continual unfolding, each cycle strengthening our wings, widening our view, and attuning us to the rhythm of the currents that carry us farther than we could have imagined.

This is what lifts us. And not just for ourselves, but so that we can become a vantage point for others.

For others, those who will stand on our shoulders, see farther than we ever could, and glimpse a horizon we were never meant to reach ourselves.

So that we may be the wind beneath their wings.

But here's the thing about the wind:
It doesn't always move in a straight line.
It doesn't always obey your plans.

At some point, you stop trying to command it, and you learn to ride it.

As you ride the wind, you may begin to notice how its invisible currents mirror the sequence you've already been moving through: Desire → Intention → Action → Result → Reflection → Evolution.

It begins with a quiet longing, the *desire* that stirs like the first breeze against your feathers. That desire sets your *intention*, aligning your wings to catch the current. Then comes *action*, the leap from the branch into open air. From that action arises a *result*, the way the wind meets you and where it carries you. In the stillness after, you *reflect*, feeling how each gust taught you, how each choice shaped you. And through it all, you *evolve*, your wings growing stronger, your instincts more attuned, your dance with the wind more graceful each time.

The wind is not just what you ride, it's the very force that moves you through this sequence, again and again, carrying you higher with each turn.

And so we arrive here, at the edge of what you thought you knew, where the currents shift, the sky opens, and the next part of the journey begins.

Riding the Currents

The wind doesn't always blow the way you expect. Sometimes it lifts you higher than you ever dreamed; other times, it strips everything away, leaving you weightless and exposed. But every gust, whether gentle or fierce, teaches you how to adjust your wings and trust the air beneath you.

When I first set out into adulthood, I thought I could chart the perfect course: accumulate all the right markers of success, and happiness would naturally follow. But the currents had other plans.

When I got married, everything I owned fit into my car. For a time before we moved into our first apartment, I stayed with my new wife in her tiny military dorm room. Over the next ten years, we built what most people would call a success story, even accumulating a seven-figure net worth. Still, I wasn't happy.

Eventually, we divorced and, through no fault of hers, I found myself with nothing. Homeless. Alone.

I wouldn't want to return to that place, but it was invaluable in my search for myself. It would take many more years, and many more experiences, before I could finally say I understood what it meant to be happy.

That season taught me what the wind had been whispering all along: no matter how tightly you grip the branch, or how perfectly you plan your flight, the currents have their own wisdom.

It stripped away everything I thought defined me, my possessions, my plans, even my sense of control, until I was forced to feel the air as it truly was, not as I wished it to be.

I've learned two things about those moments when you don't get what you thought you wanted: First, it's rarely as catastrophic as it feels at the time, even disappointment carries quiet blessings. Second, there is often something of equal or even greater value waiting just beyond your view, ready to unfold when the time is right. It may take a while to see it, but it's remarkable how often, looking back, you realize you wouldn't trade what you have now to reclaim what didn't work out then.

And in the emptiness of having lost everything, I began to notice something subtler than the strong gusts I'd been fighting.

Not every lesson comes as a gale that knocks you down. Some arrive as a quiet breeze that dances just beyond your reach, a reminder that the wind you chase isn't always meant to be caught, but simply felt, here and now, exactly where you are.

Chasing the Breeze

Have you ever tried to catch the wind? It dances just out of reach, brushing your skin, tousling your hair, only to slip through your fingers the moment you grasp for it. Happiness can feel the same way: A breeze we convince ourselves is waiting just beyond the next hill, if only we run fast enough.

We chase and chase, believing that once we finally catch it, we'll be whole. But the truth is, the breeze was never meant to be caught. It was meant to be felt, here, now, as it moves around you.

The pursuit of happiness, for its own sake, is like chasing the breeze.
It's an alluring destination, a shimmering mirage that keeps us moving forward, always just out of reach.

It's even written into the United States Constitution as an unalienable right.

But what exactly are we pursuing?
Is happiness an idea?
A fleeting feeling?
Contentment?
Or something else entirely?

I offer it instead as a state of being, not a prize to win, but a way of inhabiting your life moment by moment.

Yet we are conditioned to believe that happiness lives somewhere *out there*, beyond this job, that house, this relationship, that accomplishment. We chase it through endless milestones and accolades, hoping that if we just keep running, we'll finally arrive.

Do you want to know if you'll be happy if you get that new car, or the perfect home?

Consider if you are happy right now, exactly as things are.

I invite you to remember: there was a time that you wanted to be exactly where you are at this moment. Pause for a moment, acknowledge and honor all that it has taken and that you have given to be where you currently are.

But, If we are not happy right now, in this moment, then what leads us to believe we will be happy at some point in the future?

That "someday in the future" we've been waiting for? It's already today.

We tell ourselves that happiness waits just over the next hill, that we'll feel it once we get there.
But there is no there.

There is only here.

When we learn to walk in alignment with our truth, to speak with our authentic voice, to meet each moment fully, happiness doesn't wait for us at the end.
It reveals itself along the way.

Thich Nhat Hanh reminds us:

> "There is no way to happiness, happiness is the way."

Wind Sock

Since happiness, like the wind, isn't something to capture and hold, it's something to notice, to move with, to inhabit here and now. This exercise invites you to pause, to attune to the breeze already stirring around you, and to discover the beauty of this moment exactly as it is. Just as a windsock turns gently to show the direction of the air, you can learn to turn your attention inward and see where your spirit is already being called.

Here's a practice to help you sense the wind and orient to it, right here and now.

Let's begin:

Find a quiet place where you won't be disturbed. Sit comfortably and close your eyes for a few moments.
Take three slow, deep breaths, letting your body relax with each exhale.

Now, bring to mind something you've been chasing, a goal, a milestone, a dream, something you've told yourself:

"When I get there, then I'll finally feel happy."

Notice how your body feels as you think about that destination.
Do you feel tense? Restless? Hopeful?

Now, gently shift your attention to the step you're on right now, today, in this moment.
Ask yourself:

What beauty is here, in this step?
What truth is here, in this moment?
What can I choose to love about the journey right now?

If it helps, you can even say quietly to yourself:

> Happiness is not *there*. Happiness is *here*. In this
> step. This breath. This *moment*.

Open your eyes when you're ready.
Carry that awareness with you into the rest of your day,
remembering that the path itself is the treasure.

So if happiness is not something to chase, if like the breeze, it
can not be caught, then what *can* we pursue?

Instead of running after a mirage, we can learn to listen for
something steadier, something that doesn't dart away the
moment we reach for it.

The wind is meant to be felt, yes, but the sky still needs a point
of reference.

Just as a bird lifts its wings and rides the currents without
losing sight of the stars above, we too can look beyond the
fleeting gusts of pleasure and instead orient ourselves toward
something deeper, our own True North.

Your True North

A bird lost in a storm doesn't flail in every direction, it finds its bearings and trusts its instincts to guide it home. In life, we too are given an internal compass, a quiet knowing that points toward what is real and right for us. But it can be easy to lose sight of that True North amid the noise, the expectations, the fear.

The work, then, is not to chase the wind but to still ourselves long enough to feel that steady pull, the intuition, the direction that whispers: *this way*.

It is not the pursuit of happiness, but the pursuit of truth, authenticity, and evolution that truly matters. Being whole.

When we dare to face and resolve the blocks that obscure who we really are, when we reclaim our voice and live from the highest version of ourselves, wholeness arises.

It's a byproduct of the pursuit.

Not because we chased it, but because we cleared the way for it.

This kind of pursuit is not always easy. It asks us to confront discomfort, to meet ourselves honestly, to take full responsibility for what we've done and left undone.
It asks us to create and to share what is real, even when it scares us.

Once you've stilled yourself enough to feel that quiet pull and tap into your intuition, your True North, to clear the branches of noise and align with your path toward what's real and right for you, the question becomes:

What will you *do* with it?

Knowing your direction is only part of it.
The next step is to move, to create, to express, to embody
what you've discovered.

Just as a bird doesn't simply sit on the branch once it feels the
wind steady beneath its wings, neither can we simply stay still
once we've felt our own alignment.

This is where your dance begins, not a performance for others,
but an authentic movement of who you are and who you're
becoming.

It's not just about taking action for action's sake. Birds don't
simply beat their wings in frantic circles once they sense the
wind. They *become* the wind, meeting it with grace, intention,
and their own unrepeatable rhythm.

This is what your dance asks of you.

Not to simply move, but to move as *you.*

Not to just act, but to embody the truth you've uncovered, with
courage, with beauty, with audacity.

So now, we turn to the next part of the journey: the dance
itself, where who you are meets how you express it, and why
that expression matters not just to you, but to the sky that is
waiting to watch you fly.

Bird Dance

Every bird has a dance, not borrowed from another, but born from within. Some dance as a mating ritual, their feathers jutting and popping. Others dance in the rain, their wings raw with the memory of storms. But whether light or heavy, joyful or aching, the ballet is still theirs, and still worthy of being flaunted.

Our own dance emerges when we dare to create, not despite our pain but through it, to let it shape us without stifling us. Every move, every flit, every brave step into expression is a frolic in the rhythm of who you are becoming.

Some people seem to have ready access to this kind of expression. Their creativity flows, their hearts stay open, and joy seems to walk alongside them.

Others create from a place of deep pain, channeling their anguish into words, art, or action. There is often great truth in that kind of expression, sometimes profound truth, but it does not necessarily lead to a feeling of wholeness.

When your voice emerges only from pain, the result is often more pain.
The expression is real, but the state of being remains fractured.
Fulfillment does not come from avoiding pain, nor from marinating in it.
It comes from transforming it, using it as fuel to evolve, to connect, to step more fully into who you are.

Once we know where we're wanting to go and start planning what we want to create, something shifts.

One of my favorite reframes comes from Don Miguel Ruiz and the Toltec wisdom: the idea that *we are the artists of our lives.*

We begin to see ourselves not just as passengers, but as creators, standing before a blank canvas, with unlimited potential. The sky truly is the limit.

We get to create, as simple or as intricate as we dare. Some artists even dig rabbit holes so intricate, so layered with hidden clues, easter eggs, and meaning, that only a master fully rooted in their authentic expression could weave something so elaborate for others to delight in their discovery. Wink, wink, Taylor.

If you accept being the artist of your own life, what will you create? What would make you feel alive to share with the world?

What would you initiate if you knew you could not fail? If you took a leap and flew?

Walt Disney invites us "Whatever you do, do it well. Do it so well that when people see you do it, they will want to come back and see you do it again, and they will want to bring others and show them how well you do what you do."

I once worked with a client who dreamed of being a writer. He came to me for guidance and nearly fell out of his chair when I suggested he consider leaving his lucrative job and going for it. I didn't mean he had to quit overnight, I encouraged him to make a plan, set a date, and then, ready or not, take the leap.

I don't know if he ever did. But I do know my position hasn't changed.

Creation begins with a choice, to pick up the brush, the pen, the instrument, the courage, and to start.

I've risked everything more than once. Sometimes it worked out beautifully; other times, not so much. But what I can say with certainty is this: the lessons I've gained far outweigh anything I've lost.

For me, the willingness to risk, when it feels aligned and thoughtful, is a measure of my faith in myself. It's not about recklessness, but about trusting that I can handle the outcome, whatever it may be.

Whatever you create, be it simple or intricate, is a masterpiece when it's true to you.

When you claim your dance, when you dare to create and express from the truest parts of yourself, something begins to evolve.

The wings you've been strengthening, the feathers you've been tending, the rhythm you've been practicing, all of it readies you for what comes next.

Because the dance isn't just about moving in place.
It's about building the courage, the clarity, and the confidence to lift off.

But once you rise into the air, you'll quickly discover something else:

The sky is bigger, and wilder, than you imagined.

This is where the real flight begins: navigating the invisible currents, learning to trust your wings *and* the wind.

Once you've embodied your song and your movement, the air is waiting.
It's time to rise into it.

It's time to soar.

Soaring

There comes a moment when the branch can no longer hold you, when you realize the sky has been calling you all along. You've climbed, you've tested your wings, and now it's time to trust them.

Soaring isn't about reaching some distant horizon or chasing a finish line. It's about opening yourself to the currents that are already here, letting them carry you higher, not because you've arrived, but because you've become.

Readiness can never truly be a destination.

There is no perfect day, no singular achievement, no magical set of circumstances that will finally make you whole forever.

Life moves. You move. And destiny moves with you, when you let it arise from the way you walk, not from where you're trying to get.
It is never about arriving.
It is always about being.

And as you walk this winding road, it's natural to wonder what lies ahead, to feel the tug of fear about what might come. But there's a difference between preparing for the journey and being paralyzed by worry.

As you rise, the air feels different, thinner, freer, but also less predictable.

You begin to feel what real flight demands: trust, presence, and the willingness to meet whatever currents come your way.

Because soaring isn't only about the quiet, graceful stretches when everything flows.
It's also about how you meet the winds that whip and swirl, the ones that threaten to shake your wings or spin you off course.

Every bird, no matter how skilled, encounters both turbulence and tailwinds.
And learning to navigate them is what turns flight into mastery.

Winds of Change

Every flight encounters weather, sometimes calm, sometimes chaotic. The difference between soaring and stalling often comes down to how you meet the winds that rise to greet you.

Turbulence shakes you when you grip too tightly to fear, imagining storms that may never come. But the same air that rattles you can also lift you if you lean into it with trust. The winds aren't here to stop you, they're here to teach you how to navigate, to choose what lifts you and what drags you down.

When we worry, a couple of things happen. First, we experience the pain of what we *fear* might happen, even though it hasn't. We're essentially operating from a place of False Expectations Appearing Real. FEAR

It's true: what we fear may happen. Or it may not.

Tim Ferriss offers a helpful exercise: write your fear down on a piece of paper, tuck it into a drawer, and revisit it in six months. You'll often find the fear never materialized, or if it did, it was not nearly as catastrophic as imagined.

But here's the catch: if the thing you fear *does* happen, you'll experience the pain twice, first when you worry, and again when (and if) it actually comes to pass. And if it never happens? Then you've suffered needlessly.

It's okay, even wise, to plan. But worry is not planning. Regret (past) and worry (future) are not hospitable places to live.

So plan what you *intend* to happen. Do your part, and then let go. Step back and watch what Paulo Coelho has to share in *The*

Alchemist, "When you want something, all the world conspires in helping you achieve it."

Planning plants the seeds; worry only waters the weeds. Choose your energy wisely.

When you release the need to control every current, when you stop clinging to the fear of what *might* come, something emerges.

You realize the winds you once braced against are also the ones that can carry you, if only you let them.

The choice is no longer just about resisting turbulence or waiting for perfect conditions; it's about leaning into the rhythm of the air around you and letting it move *with* you.

Because life isn't only about mastering the winds, it's about learning to move with them, to hear the music in their flow, and to dance.

It's about learning to listen.

It was always meant to be danced with.

Dancing with the Breeze

When we first explored the idea of *chasing the breeze*, we saw how happiness slips through our fingers the moment we grasp at it, how it was never meant to be caught like a prize. But that wasn't the end of the lesson.

Because the breeze, happiness that transmutes into wholeness, is still here, moving all around us. The question now isn't how to chase it, but how to move *with* it.

For so many of us, life becomes a march toward an imagined finish line, an endless to-do list of achievements and milestones.

We forget that the meaning of a song is not found in its final note, but in how it moves us as it unfolds.

We were never meant to sprint through life with our heads down, missing the melody all around us.
The invitation is not to arrive, but to sing. Not to conquer, but to dance.

Alan Watts once said:

> *"Life is not a journey with a destination, but a musical thing, we are supposed to sing and dance while the music is being played."*

Yet even as we begin to align with that idea, it's easy to cling to what feels safe, to the familiar branches that have always held us. But the tree was never meant to carry us forever. At some point, we must trust the wind, test our wings, and see what strength they hold.

So here you are, no longer clinging to the branch, no longer just flapping, but gliding, attuned to the music of the winds.

Your dance is still yours, but now it's in harmony with something bigger.

The breeze was never waiting at the end of some distant horizon.

It's here, in the way you move through the air, in how you meet the moment, in how you let it carry you.

Not just dancing *for* life, but dancing *with* it.

And yet, even as we revel in the dance, feeling the wind lift and swirl around us, there comes a moment when the tempo softens. The music quiets, the breeze calms, and we are invited to pause.

For just as the wind teaches us to move with life, it also teaches us to listen when it stills.

When the Wind Settles

Life moves in seasons, work and rest, ebb and flow.

Recognizing that both effort and stillness are necessary helps us move through life with grace.

There are many indicators we can use to guide this process: astrological transits, the general tone and quality of the thoughts we're naturally generating, and more.

Being "hangry" is obvious. But noticing when we're frustrated or sharp with someone because we need deeper rest or reflection requires more awareness

Although it may seem simple, living our lives from a conscious place takes both intention and determination. And rest.

As a wise lumberjack reminds us:

"If my life depended on cutting down a tree in five minutes, I'd spend three sharpening my axe."

Sometimes sharpening means honing your skill.

Sometimes it means resting your hands.

When the wind finally settles, it leaves behind more than silence.

In the stillness that follows effort, you begin to notice the things that were too subtle to sense when the air was roaring, the delicate shifts, the quiet invitations, the faint patterns you couldn't see before.

Just as a bird learns not only to fly through storms but also to listen when the air goes still, you too can tune in to what's carried on the calm.

Because sometimes, when the wind grows quiet, you realize it was carrying more than just air, it was carrying whispers all along.

Whispers in the Wind

Sometimes the wind carries more than air, it carries messages. And I'm not talking about carrier pigeons. These messages are not loud or obvious, but soft and subtle, like a feather brushing your cheek. You may not see who sends them, but you can feel them if you pause and listen.

These whispers come from beyond the visible: from ancestors who still walk with you, from guides who know your soul's path, from the quiet wisdom of your own higher self. They don't shout to get your attention; they wait for you to notice, to tune your ears to the language of the unseen.

You'll only hear the wisdom of the wind if you're willing to listen.

Source, Higher Self, spirit guides, guardian angels, ancestors, these are not just poetic concepts or comforting ideas. They are real forces of love, guidance, and remembrance, available to you at all times, waiting for you to notice.

We don't always remember that we're not walking this path alone. And we don't always know how to access the support that is already at our side. But just because you can't see it doesn't mean it's not there.

Why connect at all?

Because this connection reminds you of who you truly are, not just a single person struggling alone, but a soul intertwined with something far greater.
Because the choices you face, the pain you endure, and the dreams you carry are not yours to bear in isolation.

Because when you open yourself to these energies, you begin to feel held, guided, and loved in ways that transcend the limits of the physical world.

Because sometimes what you *think* you need and what your soul *actually* needs are two very different things, and these unseen allies can help bridge that gap.

Because without connection, it's easy to feel small and lost. With connection, you remember: you're part of something vast, wise, and benevolent.

There is already plenty of wisdom out there about *how* to connect, through prayer, meditation, writing, dreams, signs in the world around you.
What I want to offer here is not the "how-to," but the "why-to."

Because the quality of the answers you receive depends on the quality of the questions you ask.

When opening yourself to these energies, consider asking:

- What would you have me see about this situation that I'm missing?
- What guidance do you have for me about this next step?
- What am I clinging to that it's time to release?
- What is the most aligned action I can take today?
- Which direction brings me closer to my truth?
- How can I honor those who walked before me by how I walk now?

You don't need to know exactly who you're addressing at first,

Source, guides, ancestors, because they already know you. Start the conversation anyway.

It's less about the form and more about the openness of your intent.
You might be surprised who, or what, answers.

As you attune to the quiet guidance already within and around you, notice what names, books, teachers, or practices catch your attention.

Guidance comes in many forms: an idea, a song lyric, a conversation, a stranger's words, a nudge toward a teacher or a healer. Pay attention to what glimmers when you're not looking too hard.

If you feel pulled toward someone or something, consider it an invitation. That pull is often your inner knowing, your intuition, pointing you toward the next guide or practice you're ready for.

One time I faced a significant choice about my future, a crossroads with profound implications. To help illuminate my path, I received a Tarot reading. The Two of Wands appeared, perfectly symbolizing the major decision before me.

A day or so later, while on a walk, I rounded a corner and came face-to-face with two stags, just as depicted on the card mirroring the choice that lay ahead. One turned and vanished into the trees, but the other remained. It stood in a literal spotlight, locking eyes with mine, unmoving, unblinking, anchored to the path that called my soul forward.

In that instant, I felt it, the clarity, the confirmation. This was my sign. The unseen had spoken, and my heart knew which way to go.

Moments like this remind us: guidance doesn't always come as words or instructions. Sometimes it arrives in symbols, in synchronicities, in the quiet certainty that rises when we're paying attention.

When you open yourself to what walks with you, the world finds a way to meet you where you are, and guide you forward.

One time, I was standing at a crosswalk when someone, seemingly under the influence of some kind of mood enhancer, ran right up to me, locked eyes with mine, and declared with utter conviction:

"It's all about love!"

I nodded, smiled, and replied, *"Yes, I agree. Now what?"*

That really is the question, isn't it?

A Zen Buddhist proverb reminds us:

> "Before enlightenment, chop wood, carry water...
> after enlightenment, chop wood, carry water."

We hear the truth, that it's all about love, but then we're still left with our hands full of wood, buckets of water, and the work of living.

So the question echoes: *Now what?*

What does love look like in this moment, at this crosswalk, in this body, in this life? How does love shape the next step we take?

Because knowing that it's all about love is just the beginning. Living it, that's the real practice.

I'm not sure it really matters what lives we may have lived before, whether we're starseeds from another planet, whether all of time is happening at once, or whether time even exists at all. Even if we're in a simulation. What matters, at least to me, right now, in this reality, on this plane, in this dimension, is *this* moment.

The one in which you, dear reader, are reading these words. The one in which your soul has chosen to be here, now.

And yes, I do believe it's all about love. Authentic love. But love is not just something you feel; it's something you live, something you extend, something you allow to guide you.

If it's all about love... then how will you choose to show it, here and now, in the small, ordinary moments that make up your day?

When you begin to listen, really listen, to the whispers in the wind, you start to notice something remarkable: you've been receiving guidance all along.

It doesn't always come as a clear voice or a dramatic sign; sometimes it comes as a feeling, a synchronicity, or a quiet nudge that seems small at first but turns out to be profound.

The more you attune yourself to these whispers, the more you see them everywhere, not just carried by the wind, but scattered across your path like tiny breadcrumbs.

At first, you may think it was just a coincidence, just a fleeting moment. But then you begin to realize: they are part of a trail, one you've been both following and laying down all along.

And so we turn to these breadcrumbs now, to notice them, to honor them, and to follow where they lead.

Breadcrumbs

Every journey leaves a trail, not always in footprints, but in quiet, shining markers scattered like breadcrumbs across time. Some were left by you long ago, in moments you can't quite remember yet still feel. Others you're planting now, with every choice, every word, every kindness, waiting for your future self, or another soul, to discover and smile at.

The path you walk is both map and mystery. You're not merely following the clues; you're also laying them down.

If you pay attention, you'll see: the breadcrumbs are already there, guiding you home.

I sometimes imagine that we are all both cartographers and travelers at once, sketching maps as we go, while also stumbling across markers we left long before, in another time, another life.

If you believe, as I do, that the soul is not limited to one single journey, then it makes sense that we would leave ourselves clues, faint, quiet reminders, mindfully placed along the path, so that when we pass this way again, we might notice them and remember.

Some of these clues are seeds we plant now, consciously or unconsciously, that may sprout long after this lifetime. (Unless they're eaten by birds! *Ha ha!*) Perhaps you speak words of encouragement to someone who carries them into the next generation, or you carve a truth into your journal that will echo in another heart, perhaps your own, someday. Or maybe you tend a patch of earth, and centuries later, the tree you planted shelters a traveler who looks up and feels inexplicably at home.

We also come across clues from before. Sometimes they may appear as déjà vu, a place you've never been feels familiar, like home. Or you meet someone and feel you've known them forever, though you've just exchanged names. Or a skill comes to you easily, as if your hands remember what your mind does not. These are the breadcrumbs we scattered in a past life, reclaimed once again.

And then there are the clues that can only be discovered here, now, in this breath, this body, this life. The way your chest lifts when you witness a sunrise. The goosebumps when you hear a certain song. The way your own words surprise you with their truth when spoken aloud. These are the reminders to stay fully awake to this moment, because the clues are not only for another lifetime, they are for this one too.

So as you walk, consider both directions at once:

- What am I leaving for myself to find, when/if I come this way again?

- And what have I already left here for myself, that inspires me, that I have yet to notice?

- And how can I honor both by being completely here, alive, now, making this life its own clue, its own masterpiece?

Notice what catches your breath.
Notice what makes your heart race or time stop or your spirit rise.

Those are the clues, placed by you, for you, prompting:
This way. Keep going.

When was the last time you noticed a sign, a symbol, a moment of synchronicity, a quiet knowing, that seemed to speak directly to you? What might it have been trying to tell you?

What seeds could you plant today that your future self, or another traveler, would be grateful and inspired to discover?

As you follow the breadcrumbs, those quiet clues scattered across your path, you begin to notice that each one doesn't just lead you forward, it also invites you upward.

They don't merely map where you've been, but hint at what you're becoming.

And if you pause long enough to really see them, you'll find they're asking you something, too, not just where are you going, but why?

Because it's the why behind your steps that creates the lift beneath your wings.

Let's step into that wind now, and explore the thermals of why that can carry you higher.

Thermals of Why

Back in *Molting Through Questions*, we explored how asking the right questions can help you shed old stories, loosening the feathers that no longer fit so that new ones can grow.

But questions don't just help you molt; they also help you rise.

Once you've shed what weighs you down, you're lighter, more able to catch the invisible currents that carry you higher. That's what these questions are, thermals of why. They lift you when you choose them wisely, when you ask from a place of possibility rather than fear.

The same mindful questioning that helped you molt can now help you soar, turning your gaze upward, offering clarity and perspective you couldn't see from the ground.

Questions are like thermals, invisible currents of warm air that lift you higher the more skillfully you ride them. But not all questions elevate; some keep you circling low to the ground, trapped in old drafts of doubt or fear.

If you want to rise, to see farther, to feel freer, you have to choose questions that generate lift. Questions that carry you toward your truth instead of anchoring you in what you already know. Remember, the power of the answer depends on the quality of the question.

The right *why* catches beneath your wings, spiraling you upward, offering clarity and perspective you could never find from the ground.

Viktor E. Frankl reminds us, in what may be one of the most profound truths ever spoken:
"Those who have a 'why' to live can bear with almost any 'how.'"

He did not offer this lightly. Frankl carried it out of the unimaginable darkness of the Holocaust, where he witnessed firsthand that those who could find meaning, even in their suffering, were the ones who endured. From that insight, he built an entire therapeutic philosophy, logotherapy, showing that our deepest strength comes from having a purpose to live for.

But purpose does not arrive on command. It does not shout over the noise of our lives. It must be uncovered, and that uncovering begins with a question.

The power of the answer depends on the quality of the question. This is no small truth. Just as Frankl's *why* can carry a person through any *how*, the right question opens the way to a deeper answer, one strong enough to carry you through storms and into light. A shallow question skims only the surface. But a worthy question, asked with openness, courage, and humility, invites a worthy answer, one that can lift you beyond the familiar and into something higher.

If the power of the answer truly depends on the quality of the question, then it's worth asking:
What kinds of questions can create thermals strong enough to carry you to the heights you're meant to reach?

Instead of asking:

How do I become happy?

Ask instead:

Am I walking in alignment with my truth?
Am I sharing my voice honestly?
Am I evolving through what I encounter?
When the answer is yes, even imperfectly, wholeness shows up on its own.

Because being happy or whole is not something you chase. It's something you create by how you walk the journey.

And how you walk, the way you speak, act, think, and show up, shapes not just your experiences, but also the reality that rises up to meet you.

Everything you put into the world carries a vibration. Your words, your actions, your thoughts, even the character you cultivate and the habits you practice, they're all energy. And they're all signals. They don't just reflect who you are, they attract what comes next.

That's why it matters to pay attention to what you're emanating. To watch what you're putting out there, because what you put out is what returns to you.

WATCH Reflections in the Sky

From high above, everything looks different, patterns that once seemed chaotic reveal their quiet order, and paths that felt invisible stretch clearly below. When you take to the sky, you begin to see how your own energy ripples outward, shaping the world you move through.

Just as birds ride the wind by instinct and intention, you are always broadcasting, through your **Words, Actions, Thoughts, Character and Habits**. These are your signals, reflected back to you like the setting sun off a still lake.

What you see in your life is often a mirror of what you've been sending out. So look closely. Watch yourself from above. Align your inner and outer skies, and notice what begins to reflect back.

And when you think the problem is *"out there,"* that thought itself is often the problem.

This is a form of projection, one of those blinking lights on your dashboard, pointing you toward unresolved energy within. Anything that deeply irks, unsettles or ruffles our feathers is an invitation to ask questions like:

- How might I show up like that myself?
- Is how I feel now how others may have felt when I acted that way?

These moments are subtle but powerful opportunities to evolve, if you're willing to explore them honestly and use them wisely.

The Law of Attraction isn't magic, it's resonance. The energy you emit shapes the energy you attract. Everything is energy, vibrating at its own frequency, and your **WATCH**, your Words, Actions, Thoughts, Character, and Habits, is your broadcast signal. It announces to the universe what you're aligned with and what you're inviting more of.

If your words are full of blame, your actions scattered, your thoughts rooted in fear, your character inconsistent, and your habits destructive, you'll likely attract more of the same chaos.
But if you watch yourself consciously, aligning your words with gratitude, your actions with integrity, your thoughts with possibility, your character with kindness, and your habits with intention, the universe responds in kind.

What you emanate becomes what you experience.

Watch closely. Choose wisely. Because you're always creating, whether you're aware of it or not.

When you learn to WATCH, to observe how your Words, Actions, Thoughts, Character, and Habits ripple through the sky of your life, you begin to see that every moment is both a mirror and a choice.

You're not just watching from above; you're also standing here, now, with the wind on your face.

It's easy to get caught scanning the horizon, waiting for the perfect breeze, the perfect conditions, the perfect *there*. But the sky is already moving. The wind you need is already here.

So before you leap toward some distant tomorrow, pause. Feel this wind. This moment.

The Wind Knows the Way

If you've ever watched a bird in flight, you'll notice, it doesn't fight the wind. It listens to it. It leans into it, adjusts to it, lets it carry, whisper, and guide, even when the path ahead isn't clear.

There's a quiet wisdom in that.

We experience something similar in our own lives, moments when we stop pushing so hard, stop resisting, and instead tune into the invisible currents already moving around and through us.

In everything I've done and in every sport I've played, I've found that same principle at work. Golf, tennis, baseball, football, racquetball, hockey, basketball, swimming, squash, they all have what athletes call *the sweet spot.*

The sweet spot is that magical point of connection where effort meets flow. It's where the swing, the shot, the stroke feels almost effortless, smooth, powerful, and precise. So much so that it feels counterintuitive at first. You're not forcing it. You're letting it happen.

And here's what I've learned: it's just one taste of the sweet spot that keeps people coming back, over and over, trying to find it again, to live in it longer, to feel that effortless connection between intention and execution.

Life works the same way. When you stop thrashing against the wind and start listening to it, when you trust the currents and find your own sweet spot, the path forward reveals itself.

The journey is not about forcing your way toward some distant destination, but about trusting the quiet currents that already know where you're meant to go.

When you let yourself move with the wind, choosing yourself, speaking your truth, showing up as you are, you discover that wholeness has been here all along, riding with you in every brave, small moment.

Practical Next Steps:

The wind invites you to listen and trust, but when it shifts or stills, here are a few ways you can meet it:

- Sit quietly and feel into your body before reacting.

- Write down what feels aligned and what feels forced.

- Pause and ask: *What is this wind inviting me to learn?*

It has never been about the destination.
It never will be.
Wholeness is what you meet along the way,
in the moments you choose yourself,
in the words you dare to speak,
in the quiet ways you share who you really are with the world.
And that, more than any destination, is worth the pursuit.

Examples of Wholeness in Practice

- A quiet **inner calm**, even when the external world is noisy.

- A sense of **congruence**, your thoughts, feelings, and actions feel aligned rather than conflicted.

- **Self-trust**, the confidence to make choices from your own truth, not out of fear or obligation.

- The ability to sit with yourself without rushing to "fix" or escape.

- Feeling connected, to yourself, to others, or to something greater, even if circumstances aren't perfect.

You'll know you're meeting wholeness not by perfection, but by how it feels to be in your own skin: calmer, more aligned, more trusting of yourself, more at home in your own life.

The journey was never about forcing your way forward, but about discovering the invisible paths that have been carrying you all along.

And now, you can feel it: the wind beneath you, the rhythm inside you, the sky calling you higher.

The next step is no longer about waiting for permission or proof, it's about listening, trusting, and stepping into what you were always meant to become.

Life, like the wind, has been carrying you all along, through still skies and storms, through resistance and release. Every choice you've made to listen instead of fight, to lean in instead of thrash, has brought you here: closer to your own sweet spot, where effort meets ease and the path unfolds beneath your wings.

You've learned to trust the quiet currents, to recognize that happiness isn't waiting somewhere "out there," but lives here, in the small, brave moments when you choose yourself, speak your truth, and dare to show up fully as you are.

It was never about forcing your way toward some distant horizon. It was about learning to ride the wind, to let it reveal the way forward, one breath, one beat, one wing-stroke at a time.

The choice is yours now, to stay, or to leap.

And so we come to the heart of it all: **Be the Bird.**

SECTION 5: BE THE BIRD

You've seen the cage, felt the weight of your stones, shed what no longer serves, and climbed higher into your own becoming. You've learned to trust the wind, to listen to its whispers, and to see the beauty in the scars and storms that shaped you.

And now you're here, at the edge of the branch.

This is the moment everything has been leading you toward: the quiet pause between what has been and what could be. The branch beneath you feels familiar, even safe. But it was never meant to hold you forever.

Below you, the ground waits. Above you, the sky calls.

Fear reminds you of the risks. But faith reminds you of your wings.

At some point, every bird finds itself at the edge of the branch, the moment between the comfort of what it knows and the vast unknown waiting beyond.

Fear whispers, but possibility answers:

"What if I fall? Oh but my darling, what if you fly?" ~ Erin Hanson

99

Ghosts of the Wind

The wind carries whispers from both directions, voices of what was, and fears of what might be.

Sometimes, as you stand on your path, you can feel them swirl around you: the echo of mistakes you wish you could undo, and the shadow of troubles that haven't yet come.

These are the ghosts of the wind, haunting you from opposite horizons.

But the wind also teaches: it can pass through you without breaking you.

You don't have to clutch these ghosts. You can let them by, and move beyond them.

Let's meet them clearly now, and discover how to release their hold.

As we walk this path, choosing, becoming, and trusting ourselves step by step, we often encounter two familiar companions: regret and anxiety.

One pulls us backward into the past, replaying what can't be changed.
The other pushes us forward into the future, imagining what might go wrong.

Both can feel heavy, loud, and relentless.
But neither has to keep you from moving forward.

Let's look at them more closely, and learn how to set them down.

Echoes of the Flight: Would've, Should've, Could've

We all carry moments we wish had turned out differently. These words, would've, should've, could've, can echo in our minds for years, even decades. Lifetimes.

Replays from the past:

"If only I could go back to high school knowing what I know now, I would've tried harder... or I should've asked out my crush... or could've have gone to that party...or not"

But here is the quiet truth:
Whatever happened was supposed to happen.
How do we know?
Because it did.

The Serenity Prayer reminds us:
God (or whatever Source you believe in), grant me the serenity to accept the things I cannot change; courage to change the things I can; and wisdom to know the difference.

We cannot change the past.
So why "should" all over ourselves?

Regret only feeds the illusion that we have the ability to change what was already written.

It drains our power and closes our heart.
It is a weight we were never meant to carry.

Currency of the Wind

Every experience we pass through leaves a trace, a transaction written in the invisible ledger of our lives. Regret tells us we overpaid. Grief insists the cost was too high. But the wind whispers otherwise: *you paid what was required, and what remains is yours to keep.*

The moments you wish you could rewrite have already been exchanged for the wisdom you carry now. You can clutch the receipt forever, insisting the trade was unfair, or you can let it flutter from your hands, trusting that no lesson is wasted, no cost paid in vain.

The wind does not chase what it has already spent. Neither should you. Let's look more closely at the currency of your past, and how to carry forward only what truly serves you.

When we look back with regret, it's often because we believe two deeply painful thoughts:
It shouldn't have happened the way it did, and *the loss was too great.*
And yet, whatever the cost of the experience... was the cost of the experience.
You paid it. You lived it.
You cannot go back to change it, nor should you live there forever.

But you *can* visit the past to glean the lesson it offered. And here's the thing: if you didn't fully receive the lesson, it's likely to repeat, and it will probably cost more the next time. Think roundabout.

We don't get to negotiate the price once it's paid. What we *do* get to choose is whether we walk away, maybe heavier, but hopefully, wiser.

Weathering the Storm

Storms don't ask for your permission, they come when they come. You can curse the wind, the rain, the lightning. You can clench your fists and shout at the sky. But none of that stops the clouds from gathering.

Acceptance is not about loving the storm. It's about realizing that fighting it only exhausts you. When you stop resisting what has already happened, when you allow the rain to fall without trying to hold it back, you free yourself to move forward, stronger and clearer than before.

The storm has already passed. What remains is up to you.

Let's explore how to release the struggle and reclaim your power.

You do not have to like what happened.
You do not have to agree with it or pretend it was what you wanted.
You simply accept that it happened.
When you say *"I accept,"* you stop wrestling with what cannot be undone.
You free the energy that has been trapped in that moment, and you begin to move forward.
Acceptance does not mean approval.
Acceptance means release.
And in that release, your power returns.

Dwelling on regret gives your power away.
Returning to the past with the intention to heal, that is something entirely different.

When revisiting past experiences, it can be healthy to ask ourselves, for future reference, what we *should*, *would*, or *could* do differently when similar circumstances arise. Not as a way to punish ourselves, but as a way to plan, to understand, and to grow more intentional for the future.

Mending the Nest

Even the strongest bird must return to the nest sometimes, to tend what's frayed, to mend what's broken, to make it whole again. The nest holds the stories of where you began, the quiet places that shaped you, the early injuries you may still carry.

To fly well, you can't ignore the splintered twigs and torn feathers that remain. Repairing your nest is not about living in the past, it's about returning with care, gathering the pieces, and weaving them into something sturdier, something truer.

Sometimes that work looks like a journey backward, retracing steps, noticing where the wound began.

Imagine hiking with a friend who gets injured along the path. You leave to get help, and then you return with the first aid necessary to address the wound.

That is a healthy reason to revisit the past, to bring healing. Resolution.

Painful memories are like the fuel gauge presented earlier, lighting up on your dashboard.
They don't light up because you failed.
They light up to say:
"Look here. This part of you needs your attention."

We don't need to revisit our joyful memories to heal them, they already shine on their own.
But moments of pain or loss deserve our attention and compassion.

Some of these moments are light, written in pencil, and can be gently erased or rewritten.
Some are heavier, written in pen, and take more effort to transform.
And some feel as though they were chiseled into stone.
These require patience, care, and persistence to heal.

And yet, even when we accept the past and begin to heal, it can still feel heavy.
We carry our memories, our wounds, our choices, and the choices of others, like stones in a pack we didn't even realize we were wearing.

Sometimes we've been carrying it for so long, we mistake the weight for who we are.
But it's not.

Let's look at what we've been carrying, and what we can choose to set down.

From Burden to Lift

Every bird knows the weight of what it carries, though not always by name. Some burdens we clutch so tightly they feel like part of who we are, hidden among our feathers. Others we've balanced so long they feel natural, almost comforting, even as they slow our wings.

There comes a time to pause, to notice the stones you've been carrying, and to decide which ones truly belong in your nest, and which are ready to fall away.

What was once a burden can become your lift, if you choose to untangle it with care.

We carry our past like a satchel of stones tangled in our feathers.
Some stones fit perfectly into our nest.
Some are smooth and familiar, worn by time.
And some are sharp, heavy, and strange, creating drag as we fly.

But the sky was never meant to be reached with wings heavy and tangled.

We feel the tug in our wings, the weight pulling us back, but we rarely stop to realize:
We can loosen those stones.
We can let them fall.

We can choose which ones to weave into our nest and which to leave behind on the ground below.

One day, another bird may gently remind you: "Squawk!"
Loosely translated as, "You can take those stones and lay them

as a perch to reach the sky you've been staring at."

When we notice and untangle the knots of our experiences, even the painful ones, we transform them into the wind beneath us.
Every stone you set down with love becomes a perch, a step, a launch point toward your highest self.

And so the stones begin to fall.
One by one, the weight you thought was yours to bear loosens and drops to the earth below.
You feel the first taste of lift, the faint, unfamiliar buoyancy of wings freed from their anchors.

But here is the quiet truth no one tells you:
The moment you feel lighter is also the moment you feel exposed.
Your wings, no longer hidden behind your burdens, now meet the wind bare, and that wind can feel strange, even frightening.

This can be where doubt takes flight.
Because letting go of what weighs you down is only the beginning.
The real test is trusting those lighter wings to carry you, even when you're not yet sure they can.

Wings of Doubt

Even the strongest wings can feel uncertain when they first meet the wind. Standing at the edge, you peer into the expanse and wonder: *What if I can't make it? What if I falter? What if I fall?*

This is the quiet language of doubt, whispering through your feathers, questioning your strength.

But every journey worth taking begins in this tension, the pause between fear and flight, between the weight of *what if* and the courage to unfold your wings anyway.

Anxiety is rooted in fear, the fear that you won't be able to handle whatever comes next.

We whisper to ourselves:
"What if the wind dies beneath me?"
"What if I lose my way in the sky?"
"What if I crash before I've learned to soar?"

But underneath it all, the fear says only this:
"I don't think I can handle it."

With this, we can look to one of the most famous birds of all time to impart her wisdom, Mother Goose. She reminds us:

"For all ailments under the sun,
There be a remedy, or there be none.
If there be one, try to find it;
If there be none, then never mind it."

And so, doubt sits on your shoulder, whispering its what-ifs, but you begin to realize: it is not the absence of fear that lets you fly, but the willingness to move through it.

The next step is not just about trusting your wings, it's about testing them.

Because beyond the edge of the branch lies more than air and possibility; there lies the fire where your resolve is tempered, where preparation meets reality, and where the true strength of your wings is forged.

This is where fear becomes fuel, and every what-if becomes a choice.

This is the crucible.

The Crucible

Once you trust your wings enough to leave the branch, the air itself becomes your teacher, and the crucible begins.As vitally important as it is to be as prepared as possible when standing on the cusp of the nest, peering out at the vast, fading horizon, ready to leap into the world, this will be far from the last leap you take. But it *is* the next one.

It is the next step into the crucible of everything you've prepared for up to this point: a rite of passage. This is where we encounter the next phase of "firsts," where survival becomes the first-place prize.

The pop quiz begins here, covering everything: hunting, nesting, evading threats, and more. Only then will we truly be ready.

Ready for what?
The next step.

For many, that means raising a family. For others, it means focusing their energy on pursuing the prey, or purpose they seek. But for all, it means coming full circle, completing the cycle, and returning to the whole.

But the crucible is not the end. It is the forge, the place where what you've prepared for is tested, shaped, and proven.

You may stumble. You may feel the heat. And you may wonder if you're ready.

And still, the horizon waits.

Because the crucible is not just about survival, it is about transformation. It reveals what you can let go of, and what you must carry forward. It reminds you that the strength you thought you were building wasn't just to lift yourself, but to lift others one day too.

And when the crucible has burned away what no longer serves you, you'll find yourself once again at the edge.

The nest behind you. The currents before you.

The next step, no longer a test, but an initiation, is waiting.

Rite of Passage: Into the Currents

Every bird comes to the moment when the nest no longer holds what it once did, the warmth has cooled, the walls feel too small, and the sky outside calls louder than the comfort within. This is not a failure of the nest, nor a betrayal of its purpose. It is simply time.

The rite of passage begins not with certainty, but with willingness, the willingness to meet the unknown on its own terms. The wind at the edge is sharper here, the ground far below more real. You are no longer rehearsing, no longer imagining the day you'd spread your wings and find them strong enough.

Here, you must leave behind the downy security of being fed and sheltered. Here, you become both hunter and homebuilder, both seeker and sanctuary. The air will test you. The first flight may be awkward, heavy, terrifying. There may even be a fall before you find the rhythm of your wings.

And yet, each dive into the current teaches something you could never learn on the branch. How to read the wind's mood. How to recognize safe shelter from subtle cues. How to navigate storms not only by avoiding them, but by rising through them.

You may fail, not once, but likely many times. You may misjudge the gusts. You might mistake a predator's shadow for your own. You could feel hunger and fatigue that the nest never taught you to endure.

But you will also succeed in ways the nest could never have shown you. You will learn to catch what sustains you. You will choose where to build and whom to circle the sky with. You will learn that survival is not just about outlasting threats, it is about weaving the lessons of each fall into the strength of your next flight.

This is your initiation. The air will not carry you simply because you've grown feathers. You must *earn* the sky by entering it, clumsy, determined, and alive.

And then, one day, when you've flown far enough and fallen enough to know both the danger and the beauty of the heights, you will look down at another trembling bird at the edge of its own nest.

And you will understand what no one could have told you: the sky was never just waiting for you to be ready.

It was waiting for you to *try*.

But even the rite of passage is not the end, it is only the

commencement of the real journey.

Because there comes a moment after the first flights, after the awkward falls and triumphant glides, when you realize: the nest is no longer your question, and survival is no longer your only answer.

You have left the comfort behind. You have learned to navigate storms, find shelter, and catch what sustains you.

But now the skies grow wider, the winds stronger, and the next horizon more distant than you imagined.

It is here, in the great expanse beyond preparation, beyond the proving ground, that you meet something new.

Not the branch beneath you. Not the lessons behind you.

Here, what carries you forward is not just skill or strength.

Here, you must unfurl your *wings of faith.*

Wings of Faith

There comes a moment in every flight when the branch beneath you fades, the sky ahead is uncertain, and the wind begins to howl its doubts. Fear flaps at your feathers, whispering: *What if you fall? What if your wings aren't enough?*

But faith begins where fear ends.

Faith reminds you that your wings were never built for certainty, they were built for trust.

The winds will shift.
The skies will darken.
And yet, if you trust the wings you've been given, you will find that they know how to carry you through.

When fear rises, it often whispers: *What if I fall? What if I fail? What if the winds turn against me?*

But the remedy is not to predict the wind, it is simply to handle it.

What if a storm blows me off course?
I'll handle it.

What if the sky turns dark and the winds rage?
I'll handle it.

What if the path ahead disappears beneath the clouds?
I'll handle it.

As Susan Jeffers writes in *Feel the Fear and Do It Anyway*:

> "At the bottom of every fear is simply the fear that you can't handle whatever life throws at you. But you can. And when you know you can handle anything, you have nothing to fear."

Regret, wanting the past to be different, is met with: I accept.

Anxiety, fearing the future will overwhelm you, is met with: I'll handle it.

You do not have to know exactly how you'll fly.
You only have to trust that you will.
Leap anyway, and trust yourself to meet whatever comes.

And remember this: you've already flown through every storm that life has sent your way.

Every detour became part of your path. Every gust and fall has shaped your wings.

And yet here you are, still soaring, still moving, still becoming.
Even the winds you feared have carried you here. You already carry what you need to meet what comes.

When we set out to learn or master something, how can we possibly know how much it will take, how long, how hard, and at what cost?

How much more?

When I first read William Blake's words:

> "You'll never know what is enough until you know
> what is more than enough"

I understood the sentence, but I had no clue what it really meant. Fluffy red feather.

It would take many experiences, many falls and rises, to realize the weight and depth of the true value of that quote. It was only then that I knew *more* than enough.

In my experience, in every pursuit, I gave whatever it took. Did I fall short?

Yes. Many. Times.
And each time, by the grace of God, or Source, I picked myself up, brushed off the dust, and resumed my flight.

It's only through not quitting, through going beyond what we thought we had, through tasting what is more than enough, that we begin to understand the measure of enough.

Our route may lead us through many iterations, but the words of Dory encourage us to:
"Just keep swimming, just keep swimming, just keep swimming, swimming, swimming!"

And boy, do I intimately know the words from poet Edgar A. Guest :

Don't Quit

When things go wrong, as they sometimes will,
When the road you're trudging seems all uphill,
When the funds are low and the debts are high,
And you want to smile but you have to sigh,
When care is pressing you down a bit,
Rest if you must, but don't you quit.

Life is queer with its twists and turns,
As every one of us sometimes learns.
And many a fellow turns about when he
Might have won had he stuck it out.
Don't give up though the pace seems slow
You may succeed with another blow.

Often the goal is nearer than it seems
To a faint and faltering man;
Often the struggler has given up when he
Might have captured the victor's cup;
And he learned too late when the night came down,
How close he was to the golden crown.

Success is failure turned inside out
The silver tint of the clouds of doubt,
And you never can tell how close you are;
It may be near when it seems afar;
So stick to the fight when you're hardest hit
It's when things seem worst,
You must not quit.

Whipping Winds

Everywhere in life, there will be contradictions. One person will say *this* is the right way; another will insist the exact opposite is true. The winds swirl, opinions clash, and the sky seems full of competing currents.

So how do we navigate the whipping winds of the sky?

After we have gathered all the information available to us, listening carefully, observing closely, we turn inward. This is why it has been so important to clear the obstacles to our own truth: because once those barriers are removed, access to our intuition becomes profound, steady, and unmistakable.

And it is equally essential to remember this: when we've made our choices, with the best information we had at the time, having sought guidance from beyond and reflected deeply within, there was no wrong choice. No mistakes. No would've, should've, could've.

There are only wins... or lessons.

And yet, even with this determination in your heart, even when you refuse to quit and press on through storms, through doubt, through exhaustion, you may still feel something clinging to your wings.

Because faith and persistence alone, as powerful as they are, do not always make us light.
Sometimes we arrive at the edge of our next horizon, triumphant in endurance, only to discover there is more to untangle.

The weight you feel now is subtler, not from the battles you've fought, but from what you've carried all along without realizing it.

You've already weathered storms. You've already learned to declare *I accept and I'll handle it.*
You've proven you can endure and overcome.

And yet, even here, soaring higher than before, you may notice a quiet drag in your feathers, a heaviness you can't quite name.

Trusting the wings you've been given is powerful, but sometimes those wings are still tangled, weighed down by what you've carried for so long you forgot it was never truly yours.

Because not every weight comes from the winds you've flown through.
Some of it was there before you ever left the nest.

It is here, in this place of hard-earned flight, that you're invited to look deeper, to see what was handed to you before you even knew you could refuse it, and to choose what you are finally ready to release.

What hidden weight is quietly clinging to your wings, and are you ready to set it down? Let's explore.

Stones & Wings

Having already begun to molt the stories and patterns that no longer fit, we now look closer, at the weight that was tucked into our feathers before we even knew we had a choice.

And some of the heaviest stones don't come from choices we made as adults, but from moments that shaped us before we even knew we had a choice.
These are the early stones, the ones slipped into our wings quietly, sometimes invisibly, long before we could name them.

Let's look at where those stones came from, and how we can begin to let them fall.

Some of the heaviest stones we carry were handed to us in childhood, long before we knew we could refuse them.

They came from moments too big for a child to understand, too heavy for small wings to hold.
They were passed to us in silence, in words unspoken or shouted, in absences that echoed louder than presence.

Some came from the way love was offered, or withheld. Some from wounds we couldn't name, but felt all the same. Others from a world that told us, in its own way: *you do not belong here.*

And so we learned to carry them, one by one, believing they were ours to keep.
We grew strong enough to bear them. We even forgot they were there, mistaking the drag in our wings for who we were.

But still, they shaped our flight.

These unspoken experiences often leave behind doubt, confusion, and limiting beliefs, stones we carry until we choose to untangle them.

Inherited Stones

These are the weights, beliefs, wounds, messages, passed to you before you knew you could refuse them.

- *A stone of perfectionism*, quietly handed to you when love and approval in your home were only offered when you excelled.

- *A stone of silence*, shaped by the rule that "children should be seen and not heard," leaving you afraid to speak your truth.

- *A stone of shame*, carved from the way a parent's disappointment fell heavier than their praise.

- *A stone of unworthiness*, slipped into your pocket by the absence of affection, making you believe you had to earn love.

- *A stone of fear*, left by growing up in chaos or conflict, teaching you to stay small and invisible to stay safe.

- *A stone of guilt*, inherited when you were made to feel responsible for the happiness or pain of others.

Borrowed Wings

These are patterns, identities, or "strengths" you learned to adopt, not because they were truly yours, but because they helped you survive or fit in.

- *The wings of the peacemaker*, borrowed from watching a parent avoid conflict at all costs, so you learned to smooth over others' storms, even at the expense of your own needs.

- *The wings of the achiever*, copied from a family culture that celebrated success but never softness, so you flew fast and high, but never stopped to ask where you actually wanted to go.

- *The wings of invisibility*, learned in a home where standing out meant getting hurt, so you folded your colors to match the background.

- *The wings of the caretaker*, picked up because no one else was there to hold the family together, so you carried everyone else, never letting yourself rest.

- *The wings of the comedian*, worn like armor because humor was safer than vulnerability, so you kept everyone laughing while hiding your own tears.

- *The wings of the skeptic*, modeled after someone who trusted no one, so you learned to guard your heart even when love knocked at the door.

Now that you can see these borrowed wings and stones for what they are, inherited weights, not your essence, you can begin to loosen their grip and decide what to do with them.

Each of these stones and wings once served a purpose: to protect you, to help you belong, to keep you safe. But now you can begin to ask:

- Does this weight still belong to me?

- Do these wings still feel true, or are they borrowed?

- What would it feel like to lay this stone down?

- What would it feel like to fly on wings of my own?

The next step is not just to *notice* the stones, but to *name* them, to hold them in the light and choose, consciously, which to keep, which to release, and which to transform into the perches and pathways that lift you higher.

The following reflections will help you untangle what's woven into your wings, so you can fly lighter, freer, and closer to who you truly are.

Stretching Your Wings

Reflections:

- What are some of the stones you remember finding tucked into your wings as a child?
- Which stones feel like they were slipped there in silence, unnoticed but heavy?
- Which stones feel so familiar you forgot you were even carrying them?
- If you could loosen and let fall just one stone today, which would it be?
- What might you build, a perch, a pathway, a launch point?

Once you've named the stones in your wings, the next step is to stretch them, to test how it feels to loosen even one, and notice the subtle lift that begins to emerge. The quiet weight that once felt inevitable starts to feel optional. You remember: these stones were placed here, but they are not you.

And as you set even a single one down, you might feel a faint lift in your wings, a hint of what it's like to rise just a little higher.

From here, something new becomes possible, a perspective you couldn't access while clutching the ground.

When you stretch your wings and dare to rise, even slightly, you begin to see yourself and your path differently.

A Bird's Eye View

When you've spent a long time on the ground, clutching your stones, or circling the same familiar skies, it's easy to forget you were born to rise.

Up close, the burdens you carry may feel sharp, heavy, impossible to release. But from above, the patterns begin to reveal themselves. The weight that once seemed to chain you has, all along, been shaping your strength.

Every scar, every stone, every story you've carried has taught your wings what they're capable of. And when you finally lift yourself high enough to see the whole path, the valleys you've crossed, the storms you've endured, the quiet beauty of your journey, you begin to understand: none of it was wasted.

The bird that soars is not free *despite* what it has carried, but *because* of it.

From this height, you can see clearly:
You are not defined by the weight you were given before you could choose.
You are defined by what you do with it now.

And as you gaze down from this higher vantage point, you realize, the stones you thought would bury you have become the very foundation beneath your wings.

Your wounding is not your fault. You are not responsible for the weight you were given before you could choose.
But you *are* responsible for what you carry now. And your healing, that is yours to claim.

If you do not tend to your wounds, you risk bleeding on those who never hurt you.

You are not broken by what you have endured, you are being shaped by it.

Every stone you examine and lay down becomes a step toward the person you are becoming.

You were never meant to live your life beneath a weight you didn't choose.
You were meant to climb higher, and higher still, building something beautiful from all you've carried.

All along, you've been gathering yourself, your roots, feathers, winds, and stones, not to become perfect, but to become whole. Wholeness isn't the absence of scars, but the presence of self. And it is from this place, whole enough to leap, that you meet the sky.

Final Blessing: The Power of Alignment

Before you take your next flight, before you step fully into the sky that's been calling you, pause here.

Take this moment to feel the quiet power already humming within you. You've shed what no longer belongs, lightened the stones in your wings, and begun to trust the wind beneath you.

Now, all that remains is to remember: your greatest strength lies in living aligned with who you truly are, and letting that truth shine through everything you touch.

Let this blessing be your breath, your anchor, and your launch, a reminder of the power you carry, and of the light you share simply by being you.

The greatest gift you can offer, to your children, your family, your friends, your community, and most of all, to yourself, is to live in alignment with your truth and to share your voice from that place.

There is *nothing* more powerful.

When you are rooted in authenticity, when your mind, body, and spirit resonate in harmony, you become a quiet force of light in the world. You emanate a vibration that uplifts everything and everyone you touch.

David Hawkins reminds us:
"One individual aligned with love and truth counterbalances the negativity of hundreds of thousands who are not."

This is the extraordinary power of a single life fully lived in truth.

And here is another truth: no matter how many candles you light in others, your flame does not diminish, it only grows brighter. Each soul you help to illuminate reflects your own light back to you, stronger and more radiant than before.

So as you stand here, between what was and what will be, I invite you to pause. To take a breath. To remember where your power comes from.

If it feels right to you, read or speak this blessing aloud, or simply let it echo quietly inside you:

Dear divine mind, body, and soul of the Creator, I ask, and give thanks and appreciation for guidance, protection, and support as I receive, integrate, and share the message of love and light with all those I come in contact. May every experience illuminate the truth, so we can access it as we navigate obstacles with grace, integrate what we learn, and evolve into the highest version of ourselves. May I share my voice from that place, with clarity and compassion, for the highest good of all. Thank you. Thank you. Thank you. I love you. I love you. I love you.

And yet, even as you rise into your own alignment, strong, clear, and radiant, you may begin to notice something else: you were never meant to fly alone forever. Alignment does not isolate you; it connects you more deeply to the flock around you. Every bird, no matter how powerful on its own, eventually meets the moment when it feels the pull of others, the call to join, to lift and be lifted. The sky is wide enough for all of us, and the journey longer than any one pair of wings can sustain alone.

The Flying V

At some point, you may realize you're ready to soar higher than you've ever flown, and even birds fly together when the journey is long.

When you feel that call, trust that the right guides, teachers, healers, and companions will appear if and when you're ready to meet them.

Don't be afraid to ask for help. Seeking support is not

weakness, it is the wisdom of the bird who knows when to ride the updrafts of others.

And when you find the one who helps you stretch your wings even wider, or when you become that one for someone else, remember: every wing that beats in truth lifts the whole flock higher.

We would never have reached the heights we've achieved without the help of others. But receiving help is not the ultimate value.

I'd like to echo what Rabindranath Tagore expressed so beautifully:
"I slept and dreamt that life was joy. I awoke and saw that life was service. I acted, and behold, service was joy."

Remembering, but not from a place of obligation, more from a place of gratitude and compassion. Remembering we are all one.

This is how you fly, not by waiting for permission, nor by clinging to the branches, but by trusting your wings, lighting the way for others, and knowing your own flame will only grow brighter as you do.

What does the bird do when the branch breaks?

It flies.
Because the confidence of the bird is not in the branch.

Be the Bird.

Questions from the Edge: A Reader's FAQ

As you close the final pages of this journey, you may notice new questions stirring in your mind, quiet as feathers, or insistent as wind at the edge of the branch.

This is natural. Questions are proof that you've been listening, engaging, becoming. They are the breeze that keeps you moving, reminding you there is always more to discover.

The following questions are ones many birds ask when they stand where you are now, between what has been and what is yet to come. They are not meant to clip your wings with certainty, but to guide you as you take your next steps into the open sky.

Remember: your journey is your own, and even the best answers are only starting points. Trust yourself to keep asking, keep noticing, and keep becoming.

How do I know if I'm ready to leave the branch?

> Readiness isn't about feeling 100% confident, it's about being willing to move anyway, even with some doubt in your wings. If you've begun to see yourself clearly, to shed what no longer serves you, and to feel the faint pull of the sky calling you forward, that is your sign.

What if I leap and fall?

You may, and that's not failure. Falling teaches you what the wind feels like, what your wings can withstand, and where your strength still needs shaping. The fall is part of the flight. You rise again, stronger and wiser.

What if I don't know what my "true north" or purpose is yet?

That's okay. The journey itself clarifies your direction. Start by aligning with your truth, choosing honesty in conversations, or saying no when something feels wrong, moment by moment: listen for what feels authentic, move toward what feels alive, and trust that the path will reveal itself in time.

How do I deal with people who don't support my flight?

Not everyone is meant to fly alongside you, and that's okay. Practice discernment: honor those who uplift you, gently distance from those who drain you, and remember that the flock you truly belong to will find you once you start soaring.

How do I know I've "become whole"?

Wholeness isn't perfection, it's a quiet knowing that you've gathered all your pieces, tended your wounds, and chosen yourself. You'll notice it as a sense of inner calm, congruence, and the willingness to keep moving even when the wind shifts.

What do I do when the wind is still and nothing seems to be happening?

The stillness is also part of the journey. Use it to rest, to mend your nest, to listen to the whispers in the wind. Growth often happens quietly before it shows itself in motion.

How do I keep from picking up old stones or stories again?

Awareness is your friend. When you notice an old weight creeping back, pause, name it, and remind yourself you already set it down for a reason. Your wings are stronger without it.

What if I don't feel brave enough to leap?

Bravery isn't the absence of fear, it's the choice to move even when fear is present. Start small. Every little leap builds your trust in your wings.

Is it selfish to focus on my own healing and becoming?

Not at all. Your wholeness is a gift to everyone around you. When you shine, you light the way for others. When you heal, you help heal your lineage. When you trust yourself, you lift the whole flock.

Where do I begin?

You already have. Reading this book, questioning, reflecting, these are your first steps. From here, listen to what stirs in you. Choose one next brave thing, however small, and let the journey unfold.

No matter how many questions you carry, remember: the answers are not always found in words, but in the way you move forward. The sky does not reveal itself all at once, it opens, one wingbeat at a time, as you learn to trust your own rhythm. Let these questions be companions, not cages, reminding you that wonder is part of the journey. When the next question arises, as it surely will, greet it with curiosity, then lift your wings and keep flying. The wind will meet you there.

About the Author

E. C. "ACE" Andersen has lived a life of rebellion, revelation, and quiet return. Born in Oakland and raised in Alameda, California, his journey has carried him through the discipline of military service, the creative chaos of acting and independent film, the exhilarating rise, and humbling fall, of businesses and fortunes, and the profound lessons of loss and homelessness. His path has been anything but linear, yet every twist has shaped his voice, his vision, and his devotion to meaning.

Today, he resides just north of Houston, Texas, embracing the role he always claimed he wanted most when he "grew up": being a grandfather, twice over so far and, of course, he hasn't really grown up.

Woven through all of it was a persistent whisper, a call to remember who and what he truly is. That quiet call carried him through trauma and awakening, through the disciplines of astrology, tarot, energy work, and intuitive guidance, and ultimately into service to others on their own journeys of becoming.

He is the Vision Steward and founder of **The 5th ACE Guidance Sanctuary**, a sacred vision taking shape dedicated to helping others reconnect with Earth, Source, and Self. Through his work at **Acetrology.com**, he helps people uncover the cards and stars they've always carried, the ones they thought were missing, and to trust the wings they've always had.

His spiritual name, **ACE**, arose as a mirror reflection of his birth initials (E.C.A.) , a quiet reminder that the 5th Ace, the one beyond the four elements, was always within him.

Described by others as *"an angel of truth who directs and grounds the light of truth, anchoring the Divine feminine within,"* he is known for guiding others toward their own truth with humility, patience, and compassion.

He would ask you this:
If the branch breaks... what does the bird do?

If you feel called to share what this book sparked in you, or if you'd like guidance on your next steps, I'd love to hear from you. You can connect with me, learn more about my work, or explore additional resources through:

Acetrology.com

Ace@acetrology.com

There you'll find ways to book a session, join the mailing list, or simply send me a note.

Wherever you are on your journey, whether still finding your wings or already soaring, know that you don't have to walk it alone.

May these words continue to guide and reflect for you, long after you close the book.
And when the branch breaks, may you remember:

The confidence of the bird was never in the branch.

Be the Bird.

With wings and a prayer,
E. C. "ACE" Andersen

Appendix: An Approach to Preening

Releasing the Stones of Childhood

Before a bird can soar confidently into the open sky, it must tend to its feathers, smoothing, preening, and untangling what has accumulated during its time in the nest. So too must we care for the early experiences that shaped us.

The following exercise is offered as a gentle way to revisit those tender, formative moments and release the weight of stories, beliefs, or wounds that no longer serve your flight.

A Note Before You Begin

Some memories or feelings that arise during this practice may feel tender, intense, or even overwhelming. That's okay, it simply means they hold meaning and deserve care. If at any point you feel too uncomfortable, unsafe, or unable to continue on your own, please pause.

You are under no obligation to complete this alone. This work can be powerful and also challenging, and it's perfectly valid, wise, even, to bring this exercise into a session with a therapist, coach, healer, or practitioner you trust.

An Invitation

Approach this with patience and self-compassion. Just as preening takes time and care, so does healing. This is not about erasing the past, but about honoring it, retrieving its wisdom, and freeing yourself from unnecessary heaviness.

Whenever you feel ready, create a quiet, sacred space for yourself and begin. You'll find the exercise on the next page.

Unfortunately, I can no longer recall where I first encountered the seed of this exercise, to properly credit its origin. Over time, I've expanded and refined it, and use this title:

Early Life Regression

Preparation: Creating Your Space

Before beginning, set aside at least 20–30 minutes where you won't be disturbed.

- Find a quiet, comfortable space, somewhere you feel safe and relaxed.
- Dim the lights or light a candle (or several), if that feels comforting to you.
- Play soft, soothing music if it helps you drop in. (Gentle instrumental or nature sounds work well.)
- You may wish to have a journal and pen nearby to note insights afterward.
- Sit or lie down in a comfortable position, perhaps with a blanket around you.
- Take three slow, deep breaths, feeling your body settle and the weight of the day drift away.

- Close your eyes if you're comfortable, and place a hand on your heart or belly to center yourself.

When you feel ready, say to yourself quietly:
"I am safe. I am here to tend to what once felt too big to face. This is a moment of healing and release."

The Practice

★ Call the Moment

Bring to mind a time early in your life that still feels painful, an experience that seems to have left a mark, or created a "code" or belief that no longer serves you.

It may have served you at the time as a way to cope, but now you recognize it as a weight you're ready to set down.

When you've chosen the moment, imagine it like a frozen frame in time. See the younger version of yourself in that scene.

★ Enter the Scene

Step into the scene in your mind's eye.
Approach the younger you gently and tap them lightly on the shoulder.
Unfreeze only them, so that you two are the only ones aware of each other.

Say quietly to them:
"I've returned to bring first aid. I'm here for you."

★ Ask What They Need

Look into their eyes and ask:

"What do you need right now?"

Wait patiently for the answer, it may come as words, feelings, images, or simply a knowing.
Then, give it to them.

If they need a hug, wrap them in your arms and hold them.
If they need you to sit beside them and hold their hand, do that.
If they want to cry, let them, and stay with them.

Keep asking gently: *"Is there anything else?"* and meet their needs until they answer no.

★ Affirm Their Strength

Once they feel tended to, let them know they *will* get through this, and that you are the living proof.

Tell them:
"What I have in my life right now exists because you endured this. You rose to the occasion. You paid the cost of this experience, and I am here to make sure the transaction is finalized."

Share something beautiful about your current life that they helped make possible, something priceless.

★ Express Gratitude

Thank them:

"Thank you for going through what you did, not because it was fair or right, but because it shaped who I've become. I will not waste what you endured. I transmute this moment into strength, wisdom, and compassion."

If you sense that this moment feels resolved for now, say your goodbyes, letting them know you may return if more healing is needed.

After the Session: Returning & Grounding

When you're ready, gently withdraw from the scene and bring your awareness back to the present.

~Take three slow, deep breaths and feel your body resting in the here and now.
~Wiggle your fingers and toes.
~Open your eyes, and look around your space to orient yourself.
~If helpful, place both feet flat on the floor and imagine roots extending into the earth, grounding you.
~You might want to drink some water or write down any insights you received.

Say quietly to yourself:
"I am here, I am whole, I am safe."

Notes:

- If you sense the moment is not fully resolved, that's okay. You can revisit it as often as you need, following the same steps.

- This process can be repeated for other experiences, each "stone" you tend to and release frees energy that can now support your flight.

When you're finished, extinguish your candle (if you lit one), and thank yourself for showing up with such courage and compassion.

When we commit to the practice of journeying back to tend to our younger selves, we engage in one of the most profound acts of self-trust and healing.

In every self-help program, training, or book we turn to, we are, at the core, searching for the truth, the truth of who we are, where our pain originated, and what it takes to grow beyond it.

No external teacher or authority can deliver that truth with the same authority and intimacy as we ourselves can.

By becoming the messenger to our inner child, we affirm that we are worthy of our own trust, capable of providing the care and honesty that younger version longed for.

This process, while simple on the surface, holds immense power: it forges an unshakable bond within, grounding us in the present and giving us confidence to walk our current path with clarity and presence. Skeptics may see it as too simple, yet it is precisely its simplicity that makes it profound; direct access to self, without filter, builds resilience, compassion, and wholeness in a way no external validation ever could.

The more we return to that younger self with truth and care, the more we liberate energy, cultivate self-confidence, and step into a life lived with grounded authenticity.

Be the Bird is not meant to be the final word on healing or self-discovery, it is the starting point. The ideas, reflections, and exercises in these pages are designed to open a door, offering a first step into a much deeper journey of self-trust, healing, and growth. In particular, the practice of tending to our younger selves lays the groundwork for an ongoing relationship with truth: the truth of who we are, where our pain began, and what it takes to grow beyond it. This is the beginning of work that extends far beyond reading; it evolves as you evolve. The book presents some tools, but the real transformation happens in the way you carry them forward, revisit them, and allow them to deepen over time. Each return to these practices liberates energy, strengthens confidence, and brings you more fully into presence. Far from being a finished product, *Be the Bird* is an invitation to continue unfolding, layer by layer, into the grounded, authentic self you are becoming.

www.ingramcontent.com/pod-product-compliance
Lightning Source LLC
Chambersburg PA
CBHW061757120626

46550CB00005B/2034